KU-499-100

# Secret Days

'*A fascinating intimate portrait of life at Bletchley Park by one who served there and who has since become one of Britain's most distinguished historians.*'
Charles Messenger

'*The first real account of Bletchley Park's human side. The crew of eccentrics makes for a very good read.*'
Dennis Showalter

'*Without doubt, this is the most important book examining the work undertaken at Bletchley Park to be published in recent times.*'
*Britain At War* magazine

'*Briggs is an engaging and amiable guide through the mysteries of wartime cryptography . . . a fascinating account of an outstanding young man and his time at a quite remarkable institution.*'
Roger Moorhouse in *BBC History* magazine

'I will keep a muzzle on my mouth with a bridle
as long as the wicked man is near me . . .
I stayed dumb, silent, speechless.'

*Psalm 39*

# Secret Days

## Code-breaking in Bletchley Park

~

## Asa Briggs

Frontline Books
London

**Secret Days**

This edition published in 2012 by Frontline Books,
an imprint of Pen & Sword Books Ltd,
47 Church Street, Barnsley, S. Yorkshire, S70 2AS
www.frontline-books.com

Copyright © Asa Briggs, 2011

The right of Asa Briggs to be identified as Author of
this Work has been asserted by him in accordance with the
Copyright, Designs and Patents Act 1988.

Hardback ISBN: 978-1-84832-615-6
Paperback ISBN: 978-1-84832-662-0

All rights reserved. No part of this publication may be reproduced,
stored in or introduced into a retrieval system, or transmitted,
in any form, or by any means (electronic, mechanical, photocopying,
recording or otherwise) without the prior written permission of the
publisher. Any person who does any unauthorized act in relation to
this publication may be liable to criminal prosecution and civil
claims for damages.

CIP data records for this title are available
from the British Library

For more information on our books, please visit
www.frontline-books.com, email info@frontline-books.com
or write to us at the above address.

Printed and bound by CPI Group (UK) Ltd, Croydon, CR0 4YY

Typeset in 12/17 point Minion Pro Medium

# Contents

For Susan
To whom *all* is now revealed.

# Plates

# Acknowledgements

I would not have been able to write this book without the help and encouragement at various stages of a small group of people. Two of them are scholarly and readable authorities on BP – Ralph Erskine and David Kahn. They read the final drafts of a book that has been long in the making, and I cannot thank them enough for their invaluable and knowledgeable comments. I also acknowledge an immense debt to Peter Lipscombe who has produced for me photocopies of crucial National Archives papers, and I thank the staff of the National Archives as warmly as I can for the help that they have given him and, indirectly, me. I append a list overleaf of National Archives papers which have transformed my own knowledge of wartime BP and how it was organized. My former colleague at BP, Ann Mitchell, has lent or given materials that have rung many bells. So too has my friend David Dilks, with whom I have often discussed my book in its making. My publisher, Michael Leventhal, has been kind, patient and unbelievably co-operative. So too has his senior editor, Deborah Hercun.

Finally and far from least, I thank Pat Spencer who has typed the manuscript through several drafts and raised necessary queries which I have done my best to answer. I feel from long experience that I can never write a book without her.

*Asa Briggs*
Lewes, 2011

## National Archives

I am deeply grateful to my colleagues in the National Archives for permission to study the following crucial papers:

1. HW 3/119, 120: the 2-volume, 556-page history of Hut Three;
2. HW 3/95–102: De Grey's history of Air sigint;
3. HW 43/1–3: Frank Birch's 2-volume history of British sigint;
4. HW 3/125: Sqn Ldr Jones's directive instructions, 401–51, for Hut Three;
5. HW 3/104: graphs and statistics illustrating the work of Hut Six;
6. HW 25/2: history of Hut Eight;
7. HW 43/70, 71, 72: 3-volume history of Hut Six, dated 29 Sept 1945;
8. HW 25/12: early Enigma history, including the pre-war meeting with the Poles and subsequent wartime correspondence between Denniston and Knox;
9. HW 14/2: Sigint matters Nov–Dec 1939;
10. HW 25/10: reminiscences by H. R. Foss on the Enigma machine;
11. HW 5/700–703, 706, 766, 767: reports of German Army and Air Force high-grade machine decrypts relating to the last week of the war;
12. HW 1/3756: intelligence passed to the Prime Minister during the last weeks of the war;
13. HW 77/1, 6: Hut Six and Hut Eight reports covering the period 1 Jan–5 May 1945;
14. ADM 223/479, section 1: memoranda by Admiral Godfrey on intelligence, security and other matters;

15. WO 208/3575: account by Brigadier Williams of Ultra as seen at the receiving end of military intelligence.

## Picture Credits

Many of the photographs in this book have kindly been supplied by Phil Le Grand and the Bletchley Park Trust. These images are Crown Copyright and used with the kind permission of the Director of GCHQ. Scans of documents and additional photographs have been taken from the collection of the author. David Kahn, author of *Seizing the Enigma*, has provided other illustrative material. Jack Copeland assisted in the preparation of some images. Additional items have been taken from the Taylor Library and a further photograph has kindly been supplied by the First Garden City Heritage Museum, Letchworth Garden City.

# Glossary and Abbreviations

| | |
|---|---|
| Abwehr | German armed forces intelligence and counter-intelligence service |
| ATS | Auxiliary Territorial Service, later renamed the Women's Royal Army Corps |
| B-Dienst | Beobachtungsdienst, the Kriegsmarine's code-breaking service |
| BP | Bletchley Park |
| BPRC | Bletchley Park Recreation Club |
| BRUSA | Britain–United States Agreement (on sigint cooperation), May 1943 |
| BTM | British Tabulating Machine Company, Bletchley |
| C | The head of the Secret Intelligence Service (SIS) |
| Callsign | A word, name or number or combination of these identifying a participant in a signals network while concealing his identity |
| Code | A system for disguising clear text, often by substituting groups of letters for common words or phrases. |
| Code book | A book, ranging from a few pages to dictionary length, containing words, letters, numbers and phrases likely to be needed for communications |

| | |
|---|---|
| Crib | Part of a probable plain text matched against an encrypted message as an aid to its solution |
| Cypher | System for disguising a text, whether in plain language or encoded, by cryptographic means, manual, mechanical or electronic |
| DMI | Director of Military Intelligence |
| DNI | Director of Naval Intelligence |
| Fish | Cover name for non-Morse teleprinter cyphers |
| Frequency | Radio frequency used for radio or other transmission |
| GC&CS | Government Code and Cypher School |
| GCHQ | Government Communications Headquarters |
| Heer | The German Army |
| Hut Three | The section of BP principally concerned with the translation, interpretation and distribution of German Army and Luftwaffe messages decrypted by Hut Six |
| Hut Four | The section of BP principally concerned with the translation, interpretation and distribution of Kriegsmarine messages decrypted by Hut Eight |
| Hut Six | The section of BP principally concerned with decrypting German Army and Luftwaffe Enigma messages, which were then passed to Hut Three |
| Hut Eight | The section of BP principally concerned with decrypting Kriegsmarine Enigma messages, which were then passed to Hut Four |

| | |
|---|---|
| Intercept | To record. manually or mechanically, a radio or other transmission |
| JIC | Joint Intelligence Committee |
| JN | American designation for Japanese Navy codes or cyphers; used with a number after the initials, as in JN-25, the main cypher |
| KGB | Soviet State Security Service |
| Kriegsmarine | German Navy |
| Luftwaffe | German Air Force |
| MI5 | Security counter-intelligence service dealing with operations inside Britain |
| MI6 | Secret Intelligence Service – also SIS – responsible for gathering information from abroad |
| NCO | Non-commissioned officer |
| NID | Naval Intelligence Division |
| OKH | Oberkommando des Heeres, German Army High Command |
| OKL | Oberkommando der Luftwaffe, German Air Force High Command |
| OKM | Oberkommando der Marine, German Navy High Command |
| OKW | Oberkommando der Wehrmacht, supreme command of the German armed forces |
| OP-20-G | US Navy's code-breaking section |

| | |
|---|---|
| Playfair | A type of cypher of British origin based on letters placed in a jumbled order in a square |
| Purple | American code-name for Japanese diplomatic Type B cypher machine |
| | |
| RAF | Royal Air Force |
| RN | Royal Navy |
| Room 40 | Admiralty code-breaking section during the First World War |
| RSS | Radio Security Service |
| | |
| SCU | Special Communications Unit |
| Sigint | Signals intelligence, covering interception, decryption and interpretation |
| Sixta | Hut Six Traffic Analysis Section |
| SLU | Special Liaison Unit |
| SOE | Special Operations Executive |
| Sturgeon | British code-name for Siemens und Halske cypher machines |
| | |
| TA | Traffic analysis of networks, callsigns, frequencies and operators' 'chit-chat' |
| TICOM | Target Intelligence Committee, consisting of British and American cryptanalysts from BP, sent to Germany after the war to collect documents and equipment relating to signals intelligence |
| TRE | Telecommunications Research Establishment |
| Tunny | British code-name for the Lorenz SZ teleprinter cypher machine |

| | |
|---|---|
| U-boat | German submarine |
| Ultra | Code-name for intelligence resulting from the solution of high-grade codes and cyphers |
| | |
| V1 | German flying bomb ('Doodle-bug') |
| V2 | German long-range rocket |
| VE-Day | Victory in Europe Day |
| VJ-Day | Victory over Japan Day |
| | |
| WAAF | Women's Auxiliary Air Force, which in 1945 became WRAF |
| WEC | Wireless Experimental Centre, British sigint base outside Delhi, set up in June 1942 |
| Wehrmacht | All three branches of German armed forces |
| WRNS | Women's Royal Naval Service consisting of Wrens |
| W/T | Wireless Telegraphy |
| | |
| Y | Wireless interception of enemy messages |
| Y Service | Signals interception organization of the three services in Britain |

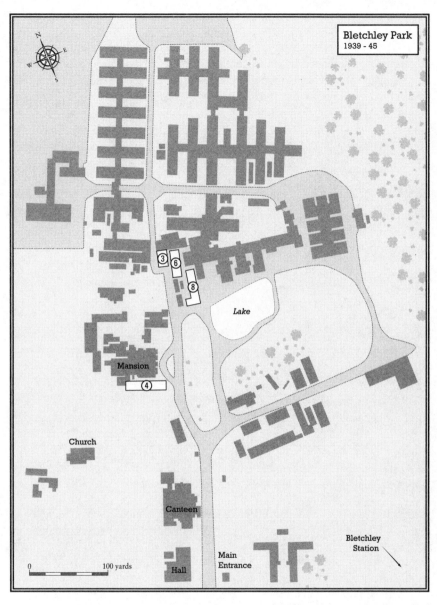

The layout of Bletchley Park changed substantially between
1939 and 1945. First came the huts, then the bombes. This plan
preceded the construction of Block D where I worked
throughout my BP days. In this map Huts Three, Six and Eight
have not yet moved into Block D.

*Chapter 1*

# BP: An Introduction

This is not just another book about wartime Bletchley Park, although it is undoubtedly that. After years of silence, voluntary and enforced, Group Captain F. W. Winterbotham was given official permission to publish his *The Ultra Secret* in 1974, and since then many books and articles on 'BP', as most of us working there called it at the time, have been published. They have varied markedly in their content and their quality, with a few of them outstanding, chief among them *Action This Day* (2001), a collection of short pieces assembled and edited by Ralph Erskine and Michael Smith. Its editors began with the statement 'Bletchley Park may well have been the best kept secret in modern British history.' They did not add that in 2001 there were a few secrets still to uncover.

I have written my own book at the end of the first decade of the twenty-first century, when it has become clear that even now there are still some secrets left, for three reasons of equal weight.

First, I am a survivor. I regard it almost as a duty to contribute a personal memoir to the collective BP inheritance while there is just time to record it. Memories are fallible and can be vague or seem trivial, but my memories of BP are not vague, and even when they seem trivial they recapture lost moods and atmospheres. By 2010 more had been written about the atmosphere and achievements of BP by people who did not work there than by people who did. For those who did no two stories are quite the same.

Second, I am by profession an historian, and I consider that it is of importance not only to recall my own experiences in perspective but to review what other writers, most of whom are not professional historians, have written about BP whether they worked there or not. BP had its pre-history as well as its history. It was a name, our name, for the Government Code and Cypher School, the GC&CS, which was created in 1919 and had its headquarters in London until it moved to Bletchley in August 1939 only a few weeks before war against Germany was declared. Its wartime history went through quite different phases as did the unprecedented volume of its work. What it was accomplishing during the 'phoney war' was quite different from what it was accomplishing when I was at BP between the early summer of 1943 and the end of the European war in May 1945.

Third, at the end of the first decade of the twenty-first century, one of the questions which I am asked most frequently about my Bletchley days is how and why did I as an historian ever work in BP at all. I was a very young historian, of course, and now I am a very old one. Whatever the reasons for a young historian being chosen as a code-breaker – and I shall set them out as clearly as I can in this book – there are certainly obvious reasons now for an old historian to write this book about the war, for most of the questions I am asked now are questions about the war as a whole and not just about BP, and I have written much about aspects of the war in other books, particularly the third volume of my history of broadcasting in the United Kingdom, *The War of Words* (1970). It was a huge-scale war different from any others.

While at BP I was just as interested in the organizational structures and operational strategies of war as I was in codes and cyphers. I was never given authority over others, but I knew well people who were. I was confident that whatever our personal interests and our personal pasts and futures might be, we shared a responsibility to do our best to help to win the war. We all depended on each other. We all had our individual contribution to make. I believed too that we should keep secret what we were doing. I was not silent because I had signed the Official Secrets Act or even because there were posters everywhere warning us that 'Careless Talk Costs Lives'.

I never anticipated then that, years after I served as a code-breaker at BP, I would be asked more questions about what I did there during a space of two years from the late spring of 1943 to VE-Day in 1945 than I would be about any other period in what has proved to be a long life. After all I was to spend fifteen years as Pro Vice-Chancellor and Vice-Chancellor of Britain's first new university of the 1960s, Sussex, and sixteen years as Chancellor of the Open University. By a coincidence – or was it more than that? – the OU, as concise an abbreviation as BP had been, was to have its headquarters in the new town of Milton Keynes within which Bletchley is now incorporated.

However many BP secrets have been revealed, there remain many misconceptions, the first of which was that the code-breakers at BP were all mathematicians. Until the late 1930s there was something of a suspicion in MI6, the responsible intelligence agency, about recruiting mathematicians to 'code-breaking'. Even after hand cyphers were supplemented by machine cyphers and mathematicians needed to be recruited, as the head of GC&CS, Alistair Denniston, clearly appreciated, some of his colleagues preferred classicists, even papyrologists. One of the most brilliant of pre-war code-breakers, Dilly Knox, born in 1884, a fellow of King's

College, Cambridge, was one of the most dedicated of classicists. I should add that I was no classicist either. Like 'Dilly's girls', as they were known at the time –and he preferred to have girls at his side – I could have said to his amusement after looking at an Enigma message, 'It's all Greek to me'.

When I moved to BP, unlike many people, some recruited by advertisement, I was asked no questions either about classics or mathematics or indeed about any of my pastimes. I did not often play chess, and when I did I played it badly. I was not interested in crosswords. People being interviewed for admission to BP, even when they were not being considered as potential code-breakers, were often asked questions about their aptitudes in these pursuits. Some were chess champions. Many could finish the *Daily Telegraph* or *The Times* crossword in their BP lunch-break – one of them was said to be able to keep the clues and the solutions in his head.

My answer to one question that I might have been asked but was not would have been relevant. Nobody at BP knew that when I was twelve I had invented my own language, Aotics, that was based on a code. 'Based on' are two words that I have deliberately chosen. I occasionally superimposed on the code my own linguistic rules. I was writing cypher and code when I occasionally used Aotics in entries in my childhood diaries. That, I believe, would have been considered a qualification for code-breaking in BP had anyone known about it.

Code-breakers were in a small minority in wartime BP, which grew to be a sizeable organization by any standards. It is another misconception that they were in the majority. A multitude of tasks were performed at BP, all of them necessary if German and other codes were to be broken. When I moved to BP in the late spring of 1943 there were no fewer than 2,640 civilians and 2,430 servicemen and women working in BP and its scattered out-stations, all of which belonged to the same complex. We depended on them as much as on people working in BP.

Even among the code-breakers, not all of them worked on machine cyphers. Nor was Enigma, an evocative name, the only machine cypher. A common misconception is that when the computer Colossus was built, a remarkable achievement, it was involved in breaking Enigma. It was not. Sophisticated teleprinter cyphers, unromantically labelled 'Fish', needed increasingly sophisticated machines to tackle them. Colossus was supreme among them. The bombes which were built to help break Enigma were not computers. They were electromechanical machines built outside BP at Letchworth and later in the United States. They were housed mainly at out-stations like Wavendon and Gayhurst. They were operated by the WRNS, the Women's Royal Naval Service, and their operators were usually called Wrens.

Almost everything that BP did depended on radio interception without which there would have been no cyphered Italian, German or Japanese messages to 'break'; and while it is only recently that interceptors, many of them volunteers, have been given the tribute they deserve, I admire Gordon Welchman, a mathematician who will figure prominently in this book, for laying emphasis at the time, and in his book *The Hut Six Story*, on the importance of what they were doing. It was obvious that translators were always needed too to pass on messages decrypted by code-breakers and translated into intelligible English to people making use of them outside BP in Whitehall or in operational commands.

Almost as obvious was the fact that Ultra intelligence, as it came to be called in 1941, had to be sifted, summarized, registered and indexed. BP always demanded team effort. With the minimum of bureaucracy nearly ten per cent of the total workforce at BP in January 1945 was employed in what was described as 'administration'. There were also no fewer than 152 cleaners, handymen and watchmen, 151 maintenance workers, and 139 catering staff. Transporting people who were usually working on a shift system was an essential service, and there were 79 men and 560 women drivers, using no fewer than 137 vehicles of many different types, including 40 coaches.

Such numbers were not untypical of organizations that grew fast during the war years. Yet there was a special place in BP for brilliant individuals, some of them eccentrics like Alan Turing and Josh Cooper. Turing had so many eccentricities that they seemed to everyone who saw him weird signs of genius. Cooper, tall and burly, was described by Aileen Clayton, then a young WAAF signals intelligence operator, as 'one of the most unforgettable people she had ever met . . . slightly deaf, incredibly unkempt in his dress, dark hair flopping over his face'. He seemed to know everything that was going on in BP.

Such knowledge was rare inside BP. Some of the people who were indispensable to the breaking of messages transmitted in the German Enigma machine cypher were never even told that it was being broken nor, indeed, just what part they were playing in what for many of them was a boring routine process. Some of them, including 'debs', who were never in short supply at BP, felt that what they themselves were doing was incomprehensible and had no notion of the end product of their work. Some of them felt that they were cogs in a machine. Stuart Milner-Barry, pre-war chess correspondent of *The Times*, who was placed in charge of Hut Six in 1943, the highest post he could have held at BP, was more nervous about the monotony of the work that the girls were doing than in their sometimes ill-disguised feelings about BP.

There were other inmates of BP who felt that the time they were spending at BP constituted the golden years of their lives. This usually had less to do with work than with the sense that they had of belonging to a genuine community. The Park was a sociable place. As one of the WAAFs recruited in 1942, Gwen Davies, put it memorably in a book published in 2006, *Cracking the Luftwaffe Codes*, for which I wrote an introduction, 'to be with people for whom books, music, art, history, everything like that was a daily part of our lives, it was an absolute blossoming'.

People wrote poems at BP as well as read them; one of the most remarkable poems was Henry Reed's 'Naming of Parts', first published before he arrived in BP in a wartime edition of the *New Statesman*. In October 1944 Gwen married the Welsh poet Vernon Watkins, whom I knew well at BP. He had arrived in BP before me. His head of section told him hopefully that he should not write any more poems while serving in the RAF to which he replied that as a matter of fact he wrote poems all the time! Vernon was a friend of Dylan Thomas, who seemed to me to make poetry live again. I felt while at BP that 'what poets wrote about war was far more important that what historians wrote'. There were several historians at BP who themselves wrote poems. I was one of them.

Looking back, the two years I spent at BP were not the golden years of my own life, as they were for some of the men and women working there, but I never believed myself to be a cog in a wheel in any sense, and while at BP I felt privileged to be helping to make history. Later in my life, as I shall explain in my penultimate chapter, I was left with far more than a sheaf of purely personal memories, which for decades we had to keep to ourselves. I had changed my ways of thinking and feeling.

Whatever we were doing at BP we were pledged to secrecy. In my own case my mother, father and sister did not know anything about what I was doing there, although they knew that I was working in a place called Bletchley and sent letters to me addressed Bletchley, Box 101. My sister occasionally visited me. When I got married ten years after the war I did not tell my wife what I had done at BP. Occasionally at a party or in the street the two of us would meet someone who asked me whether I had recently seen any of 'the Hut Six lot', and Susan would ask me what Hut Six was. I would give her the briefest of answers.

Some of my colleagues at BP were even more secretive than I was. For example, for thirty-five years Oliver Lawn, who worked with me in Hut Six, had not talked to his wife Sheila, who had worked in a different part of BP (they married in 1948), about what he had been doing. Nor did she tell him what she had been doing before or after they met. Their tongues, they felt, were bridled, but they did not complain. Once many secrets had been revealed they returned happily to visit post-war BP where they learned things that neither of them had known when they were working there. They were then also told about things that they had once known but had subsequently forgotten.

In now telling my own story I draw on other people's stories, like theirs, for there was much that mattered in BP which I did not know of at the time, for example, about double agents and the Abwehr, the German secret service, which I have learnt about since. Doubtless there is a lot that I still do not know. I do know, however, through my own story, more about radio interception than historians concerned mainly with cryptography. I was a member of the Royal Corps of Signals before I was a member of the Intelligence Corps. Having worked briefly in the Y Service, which I did not identify as such, before going to BP, I was already fascinated by direction-finding and the intricacies of traffic analysis.

I have subsequently read with interest Kenneth Macksey's *The Searchers: Radio Interception in Two World Wars* (2003) which he rightly sub-titled *How Radio Interception Changed the Course of Both World Wars*, and Hugh Skillen's *Spies of the Airways* (1980) and *The Y Compendium* (1990). Skillen, commissioned in 1941, had joined the wireless intercept branch of the Intelligence Corps, and in 1942 had been appointed officer commanding a wireless intercept section attached to the US Army. He worked at BP from 1943 to mid-1945. He and later his wife Jean arranged particularly illuminating 'Enigma Symposiums'; the first two of them in 1992 and 1994. They drew in contributors from various parts of the world. Skillen's enthusiasm was as impressive as his knowledge.

Even when I read Welchman's *The Hut Six Story* I did not realise there had been many heated wartime arguments about the organization of the Y Service and, indeed, of sections of BP. I knew at the time that there had been serious personal frictions in Hut Three before I arrived. Recently Christopher Andrew's *The Defence of the Realm* (2009), subtitled *The Authorized History of MI5*, was followed up by Keith Jeffery's *MI6: The History of the Secret Intelligence Service, 1909–1949* (2010) which, however, devotes little attention to BP. Andrew, the doyen of intelligence history, is a fellow of a Cambridge college and a professor of the University. My main source of knowledge consists of 'primary sources', some of them indispensable, now kept in the National Archives, which I have gratefully listed in my acknowledgements.

Tensions and frictions have been identified at an even higher level than intelligence, for example, in Andrew Roberts's *Masters and Commanders* (2008), which is sub-titled *The Military Geniuses who led the West to Victory in World War II* and which draws on many sources. The press had picked out one of the published sources seven years before. When Lord Alanbrooke's unexpurgated diaries appeared in 2001, they were serialized by the *Sunday Telegraph* under the headline 'Britain's Wartime Military Chief Thought Churchill "A Public Menace"'. Retired American military chiefs had been asked in the early 1970s if they would be willing to be interviewed for an oral history project. What they told their interviewers constitutes a treasure trove of unexpurgated anecdotes and reflections.

I have already noted that I am asked more questions about the time I spent at BP than about any other period in my life. The questions fall into three categories. First, people ask me about celebrities whom they have read about elsewhere, including people as different as the retiring but admired BBC story-teller, 'A. J. Alan' (Leslie Lambert), and the flamboyant novelist Angus Wilson, who disturbed his BP colleagues by his dress and his manners. The *dramatis personae* of BP invites curiosity. There was always a sense of a stage with many players.

Second, and more numerous, are questions relating to members of the questioners' own families. Did I know X or Y at BP? What details can I give about them? Usually I reply 'No' to such questions, not surprising in that at its peak there were around 10,000 people working at BP. Annoyingly there is no complete list of the names of people who worked at BP or what they were doing. A BP *Who Was Who* would be extremely useful. Sometimes I am surprised by my own discoveries. In the course of carrying out research on this book I have found that there were people I knew before or after BP whom I did not realise had ever worked there.

An excellent recent book by a colleague of mine at BP, James (we called him Jimmy) Thirsk, *Bletchley Park: An Inmate's Story*, published in 2008, the kind of history that I am trying to write myself, includes valuable brief biographies. I now appreciate more fully than I did before reading Jimmy's book that Winterbotham, whose text was vetted by 'the authorities' before publication, was not the first Englishman to break the taboo on secrets. Indeed, six years before writing about BP at length, Winterbotham had referred generally in his book *Secret and Personal* to 'the role played by our most valuable and reliable source of intelligence in a few of the vital turning points of the war'.

Even earlier, in a book review of January 1967, the journalist with an unforgettable drawling voice, Malcolm Muggeridge, a former MI6 officer, seems to have felt no responsibility for keeping secrets. He referred without naming it to 'a country house where the Intelligence department concerned with code-breaking had succeeded in cracking the German military cyphers – a terrific and for security reasons, little known feat, never before, to the best of my knowledge, pulled off on anything like the same scale'. In a later review in *The Observer* of 2 April 1972 Muggeridge went so far as to name the house, 'Bletchley'. Not a professional historian, he had used somewhat disparagingly the term 'an infusion of amateurs' in his first review, and in his second he mentioned code-breakers playing rounders 'to refresh themselves for their arduous labours'. Any playing of rounders had longed ceased before I went to BP, but I did know that Churchill himself had arranged for new tennis courts to be prepared for BP's inmates.

It was nevertheless a professional historian, Hugh Trevor-Roper, later Lord Dacre, who, first in articles in *Encounter* and then in a book on *The Philby Affair*, published in 1968, called GC&CS an 'imperfect organisation', while describing 'the breaking of the Enigma machine' as 'the great intelligence triumph of the War'. Trevor-Roper, author of *The Last Days of Hitler* (1947), had worked in a different branch of wartime intelligence, RSS, the Radio Security Section, which was transferred from the War Office to SIS in May 1941, as I describe in a later chapter.

The Soviet agent Kim Philby, whom he knew in SIS, gave him a good lead-in to a more general discussion of organization and policy. Philby himself knew only too well how to keep secrets, as, of course, did Stalin whom he faithfully served. Journalists did not seek deliberately to expose secrets in the 1960s as they do today, but I knew then, long before Winterbotham, that at least one mass-circulation American publication, *Time* magazine, had given the basic facts away. I keep old issues of *Time* in my own archives and have a copy of the number of 17 December 1945 which reported that the Americans and the British had been breaking German and Japanese codes and cyphers during the war. It did not say where.

In 1968, when it came out, I bought David Kahn's great book *The Code Breakers*, 1,164 pages long, which went back to the beginnings of cryptography and suggested at the end that 'a foolish secrecy still clothes much of World War II cryptology'. 'To tell that story in full', Kahn admitted, 'would require a book the size of this.' He mentioned what the Foreign Office 'euphemistically called its Department of Communications', locating it in BP. Perhaps surprisingly, none of the Americans who worked with me at BP and with whom I was still in touch after 1945 referred to the *Time* article, or indeed to the massive Kahn volume.

The first person outside BP to whom I revealed any of its secrets was Ronald Lewin, a friend of mine high up inside the BBC, whose *Ultra Goes to War: The Secret Story* (1978), was the best of the books that were published about BP during the 1970s. I had been greatly impressed by Lewin's life of Field Marshal Slim, which won the W. H. Smith Award in 1977, and I believed that the first unofficial history of BP should be written not by an insider, like Harry Hinsley, but by an able and distinguished military historian who approached BP from outside.

In writing this present book, I looked back in my own archives at a letter written to me by Lewin on 10 March 1976:

> You will be amused to know that the germ that was sown [did I sow it?] right at the end of our pleasant lunch together has subsequently sprouted like mad. That is to say, all the ideas I had been gathering about Ultra suddenly came into focus during our conversation, as you saw, and I am now committed to write for Hutchinsons before the end of next year a book which I have provisionally entitled *The Ultra War* . . . Please may I have a proper talk with you about Bletchley in terms of your own experience. You will understand that I would not wish to push you any further than you may want to go.

I am now belatedly (and in retrospect) meeting Lewin's request, still unwilling, after so much has been written about BP, to push further than I should. I note, too, that Lewin added in his letter 'I can only [write any book] by talking to chaps like yourself since the main documents are not likely to be available, I suppose, until Harry Hinsley's Official History sees the light of day – if it ever does.' And PS, in ink, 'this of course, won't do what I hope to do – which is to relate Ultra to the commander's mind, to the actual process of fighting the battle'.

The five volumes written by Harry Hinsley (and others), *British Intelligence in the Second World War* (1979–88), need to be read by all historians, both of intelligence and of the war. Hinsley, born about a fortnight after the First World War, who arrived in BP as a young historian from St John's College, Cambridge, in December 1939, could never have foreseen that one day he would be writing them. Nevertheless, given the key role that he played in BP, he was uniquely qualified to do so. Three years older than me, he had not yet taken his degree in 1939, but in BP he quickly developed naval intelligence and ended the war as assistant to Commander Edward Travis, by then the head of the whole of GC&CS, who was thirty years older than he was and who during the First World War had served on the personal staff of Admiral Jellicoe.

In 1979 Hinsley became head of his Cambridge college, St John's, and from 1981 to 1983 he was also Vice-Chancellor of Cambridge University. I never talked to him about BP after the war or reviewed any of the volumes in the official history, nor indeed any of the early books on BP, preferring to keep my own secrets as most of my contemporaries did. I noted, however, that he had been told not to include names of people in it. Subsequently Maurice Oldfield, a former Director of MI6, whom I knew, told me that he felt that the volumes left an impression that 'the intelligence war was won by committees in Whitehall'. Ironically it was in observing Hinsley's own life after BP that I realized that we have to study the whole lives of people who mattered at BP, including what they did at BP and after, as well as before they arrived there.

Official histories require even more critical scrutiny from their readers than personal accounts of life in BP, for although there is formidable research behind them, even at their best they present history from above, not from below. A later book edited by Hinsley himself and Alan Stripp, *Codebreakers: The Inside Story of Bletchley Park* (1993) is a far more lively (and revealing) 'read' than his official history. The liveliest personal account of all, which deals with far more than BP, was R. V. Jones's *Most Secret War* which appeared in 1978. I myself talked to Professor Jones about BP and its personalities several times many years later, somewhat surreptitiously, on visits to Aberdeen University when he held a chair there and I was a member of the University Grants Committee.

The more we talked, the more I was left in no doubt that Jones knew far, far more about BP than I did. Summoned into the Air Intelligence branch in 1939, he made his first visit to BP in September 1939, where he spoke to Travis as well as Josh Cooper and, curiously, A. J. Alan. Indeed, I felt and still feel that Jones knew more than Hinsley did about all aspects of 'intelligence', a term which, as both of them have explained, it is not easy to define.

The third category of questions about BP are those which I would myself like to have asked, particularly of academic historians who worked at BP. In particular, I wish that I had talked to my fellow historian Ralph Bennett, seven years older than Hinsley, a major in the Intelligence Corps and for twenty-seven years after the war Director of Studies in history at Magdalene College, Cambridge, ending as its president from 1979 to 1982. In 1979 he published the first of four volumes on the wartime use of BP intelligence, *Ultra in the West: The Normandy Campaign, 1944–1945*. Ten years later, free from the mastership of Magdalene and living at Kew, near to the Public Record Office, he published *Ultra and Mediterranean Strategy* (1989), followed by *Behind the Battle: Intelligence in the War with Germany, 1939–1945* (1994).

Two years after that he published a collection of articles and lectures on intelligence called *Intelligence Investigations: How Ultra Changed History* (1996). Bennett had studied medieval history in Munich before the war, and I was one of a handful of undergraduates who heard his first lectures on the subject early in 1939. The main subject which I would like to have talked about with him was not how the Germans were re-writing medieval history in 1939, but how they responded to his own volumes on twentieth-century history, and how they themselves evaluated BP when they began to hear about it.

This is still a subject which demands research in depth, and David Kahn has already turned to it. I know from him what kind of enquiries the Germans made during the war about the security of their own cyphers, prompted largely by Admiral Karl Dönitz. Designated as Hitler's successor in 1945, the admiral figures prominently in Chapter 8 of my book. I have read and admired the German historian Professor Jürgen Rohwer's researches, particularly on the U-boat war, which has also been at the centre of Kahn's studies. He founded in 1993 the Arbeitskreis Geschichte der Nachrichtendienst, which became an international body, the International Intelligence History Association, in 1999; and in the same year in the *Journal of Military History* he described 'Signal Intelligence and World War Two' as an 'unfolding story'.

It would have been valuable to read German reviews concerned with the role of intelligence in military campaigns between 1939 and 1945 and of the work of Bennett in particular. Nonetheless, there is only one gap. I have not been able to find any German reviews of Gordon Welchman's book *The Hut Six Story*, which first appeared in the United States in 1982 in a very different form from its later editions. I shall not only pay my personal tribute to Welchman in this book but draw on his indispensable chronology of the different phases of Hut Six history, which he set out in 1982 and modified four years later in an important article, 'From Polish Bomba to British Bombe: the Birth of Ultra'.

A reliable chronology is necessary in all histories, whatever their coverage, but Welchman, close to the centre of power in BP, who was a far better historian than many of its professional historians who have tried to tell its history, had been in no position to understand the importance of Poland in the history of Enigma before he read an English translation of the brilliant Polish cryptanalyst Marian Rejewski's 'How Polish Mathematicians Deciphered the Enigma'. Dilly Knox had not chosen to tell him how when Welchman arrived in BP in September 1939.

Welchman stayed in BP from the beginning to the end of the war, and whatever he was told or not told he very quickly reached the conclusion that, in the new kind of war that was just starting, BP would have to deal not just with the breaking of individual messages but with the total output of an intricate communications system. He learned more about it, myths and facts, later in the war when Travis sent him across the Atlantic on the *Queen Mary* in 1944 and he entered 'the strange world of Sir William Stephenson', 'Little Bill', a millionaire businessman born in Canada, who had been appointed British liaison officer with the American intelligence services in May 1940.

As a go-between, trusted by both Roosevelt and Churchill, Stephenson had his headquarters in the middle of New York in the Rockefeller Center, where he lavishly entertained people whom he thought would be of use to him as the head of British Security Co-ordination (BSC). The error-ridden biography by a different Stevenson (spelt differently) described him (incorrectly) as the 'Man Called Intrepid'. That was only the name of BSC's cable address. After the war I got to know the Rockefeller Center well. It was the headquarters of the Rockefeller Foundation, which paid my costs to travel round the United States for the first time in 1952, and it was also the BBC's major American office, the head of which had his title changed in September 1941 from Representative to Director. I had done no work at that time on the organization and history of broadcasting but when I began to do so during the late 1950s I spent much time travelling up and down its giant numbered elevators.

Within BP I was never directly concerned with the analysis of intelligence, yet I crossed the threshold of Hut Three, the intelligence hut, almost every day and got to know many of the people who were working there. Some I got to know very well after the war, including Jim Rose, who was to marry Pam Gibson, who also worked at BP, arriving from the theatre and returning to it late in her life. Pam was the sister of a close friend of mine after the war, Lord Gibson, who was to be chairman of both Penguin Books and of Longman, the oldest publishing house in the country, about which I later was to write a comprehensive history.

Rose's colleague, Peter Calvocoressi, for a time chief executive of Penguin, was to join Sussex University as Reader in International Relations. Within the context of this book, however, he is important in that he was to write one of the most readable short accounts of BP, *Top Secret Ultra*, in 1980. This focussed on the sheer range and volume of 'intelligence' handled in Hut Three.

After the war, in the late 1940s and early 1950s, I discussed military intelligence with Brigadier E. T. Williams, Montgomery's former intelligence chief, whose appointment as a fellow of Balliol was announced in *The Times* in 1944, simultaneously with my appointment as a fellow of Worcester College, Oxford, and naval intelligence with Captain S. W. Roskill, who published his book *The Navy at War* in 1960. A memorandum by Williams on the use of Ultra in the field in military operations (WO 208/3575), labelled Top Secret, is one of the most interesting documents on the subject produced during the war.

I had rather fewer personal contacts with individuals in Hut Eight, the section breaking naval Enigma, than with individuals in Hut Three, although I knew that Michael Ashcroft left Hut

Eight in 1944 to work not on Enigma but on the very different group of cyphers called Tunny (from the Fish set), as Roy Jenkins was to do when he arrived in BP in April 1944. Sadly in retrospect, while Ashcroft and Jenkins were working on Tunny I talked with them far more about economics than cryptography, which was a taboo subject. I had seen a lot of Shaun Wylie when he was in charge of Hut Eight's Crib Room, and of Hugh Alexander, who played chess for England and was a friend of Milner-Barry and was with him playing chess in Buenos Aires when war broke out. Alexander was briefly in Hut Six at BP before moving to Hut Eight, becoming its head after Turing.

There were close operational links between Huts Eight and Six since we were all involved with the same cypher system, Enigma, and we all depended on easy access to meticulous indexing, an essential component in all code-breaking. I knew little, however, about Hut Four. In general, while I was at BP I knew rather more about what was going on in other parts of BP from mine than most people did who were working in other sections, but I was not encouraged to find out too much. Fortunately, I always had many personal contacts with people working on Japanese codes and cyphers. I first met some of them on a Bedford Japanese course before I arrived in BP and a few of them became close friends.

A mutual friend outside BP had told me that Jenkins was on his way to BP before he arrived there but I did not know that he was to work not on Enigma but, somewhat unhappily, on Tunny cyphers. In the light of all this, I have become very critical of the many quite sophisticated recent accounts of BP that suggest that breaking Enigma was the only significant BP achievement. I am equally critical of accounts that imply that distinguished late entrants to BP often worked there for a far longer period of time than they did.

I realise now, of course, in the light of all the books that have appeared since the 1970s, some of them highly detailed studies, that much was always going on behind the scenes at BP about which I knew nothing and that there were key figures in the story of BP whom I never saw, let alone met. For example, I scarcely met Mavis Batey (in 1939 Mavis Lever), born two days before me in 1921, and her husband Keith, who died when I was beginning to write this book. Their paths did not cross mine until after the end of the war in Oxford, when Mavis was well known as a conservationist and expert on garden history and when Keith was involved in college and university finance.

The Abwehr Enigmas, which Mavis has written about in many places, were totally unknown to me at BP, although they were the mode of communication of some of the most important strategic messages that the Germans sent. I have enjoyed talking to Mavis about her experiences at BP and reading what she has had to write about them, particularly her account of the Battle of Matapan.

While the battle was being fought between U-boats and convoys in the Atlantic the Italian fleet in the Mediterranean was decisively beaten at Matapan in March 1941 in a battle in which Ultra played a decisive part. Hut Eight was not directly involved. It was Dilly Knox's section in 'The Cottage' at BP which, on 27 March 1941, forwarded a message to Admiral Cunningham's flagship in Alexandria warning him that the Italian Navy planned an attack on a British military convoy carrying troops from Egypt to Greece to help the Greeks defend their country against the Germans. Ultra turned an Italian attack into a British attack which effectively put the Italian Navy out of action. In Churchill's words it was 'the greatest sea fight since Trafalgar'.

There were fascinating twists to the narrative. The Ultra message was sent not via Hut Six and Hut Three, although they had provided Cunningham with vital information earlier. The Knox message was sent by Mavis Batey, one of his remarkable Dilly girls. It was received on the flagship *Warspite*. E. H. Lee, the officer who decoded the signal, had never heard of Ultra and was warned by a lieutenant-commander to place the information on the admiral's strategic chart in his cabin and to bring the signal back at once 'under pain of death'.

Now came a brilliant piece of deception on the Admiral's part. It was known in Alexandria that he always sailed with his fleet, and now he pretended, with the Japanese consul, a known spy for the Axis, observing and eavesdropping on him at the golf club-house of the Alexandria Sporting Club, that he was giving a dinner party ashore that evening. He even carried his dinner uniform with him. The Japanese consul passed on the information, and as soon as darkness fell the Admiral sailed off with his fleet, moving to the spot specified in the Ultra message.

The final twist to the story is that the future wife of E. H. Lee, the first recipient of the Ultra message, worked with A. R. Bradshaw, BP's administrative chief, for three years. Cunningham on his return to England visited BP and in person congratulated Dilly's girls. He was accompanied by the Director of Naval Intelligence, Admiral Godfrey. Cunningham toasted the girls in wine brought at the Eight Bells down the road from BP.

Dilly Knox had himself broken the K-Enigma, which the Italians had used and Dilly had broken during the Spanish Civil War. He was helped to send his message of 27 March 1941 direct to Cunningham's flagship by his pre-war friend and colleague in Room 40, Nobby Clarke, who, fortunately for Knox, was then head of the Italian naval section. Clarke wrote his own splenetic account of life in BP, where he resisted the rise of Frank Birch. The gifted Clarke and Knox objected to cryptographers being kept in the dark about intelligence which as part of Welchman's plan was concentrated in Huts Three and Four. After Knox had broken the German Abwehr cypher he had insisted that Denniston, still in command, should name his section ISK – Intelligence Section Knox. Peter Calvocoressi of Hut Three described Knox's conveyance of the message direct to Cunningham's flagship in March 1941 as 'one exception to the rule'.

I have also enjoyed talking to Churchill's biographer, Martin Gilbert, whose book *The Second World War*, which surprisingly does not figure in Andrew Roberts's bibliography, is the only general history of the war which fully integrates intelligence history into military history. He has also written detailed studies of particular periods in the history of Enigma and of Churchill's assessment of its importance. I note in my last chapter that there is a fascinating collection of Churchilliana at BP that was assembled by Jack Darrah with no particular reference to cryptography.

While in Hut Six I managed to do some writing of my own on the history of the Second World War. In my spare time at Bletchley, insofar as there was any, I co-authored a well received book, published in 1945, called *Patterns of Peacemaking*. One of my two co-authors, David Thomson, then a research fellow of Sidney Sussex College, with whom I first discussed the project, subsequently became master of my old college. I used to slip over to Cambridge to see him in 1944 and 1945 and to discuss our text, but I never mentioned any details of my working life at BP to him except to inform him that I had a typewriter there. The framework of that wartime book, like the framework of this book, is clear from its contents page.

In this book I start with Cambridge, where I was an undergraduate of Sidney Sussex College from 1938 to 1941, and I end with Oxford where I was elected a fellow of Worcester College in the late summer of 1944 and where I stayed until 1955, returning again as provost from 1976 to 1991. The framework may suggest that in my experience and attitudes I am thoroughly 'Oxbridge', to use a term I intensely dislike. In fact, many of the most interesting, indeed exciting, times in my academic life have been at other universities, beginning with Chicago, the university that taught me most, and the Institute of Advanced Studies in Princeton, headed in my time there by a besieged Robert Oppenheimer, who kept more secrets than I ever did, and who to the end of his life never fully disclosed the details of his own wartime story.

It was through BP that I first encountered Americans, including American academics turned cryptanalysts, and I discuss their role in this book. I had met no Americans before the start of World War II and at BP I was far from alone in this. I was lucky to meet Telford Taylor, the first American officer to establish effective liaison with BP on the army and air force side. He had joined the Special Branch of the US Army Intelligence Service as late as August 1942 and arrived at BP in the late spring of 1943, where he shared an office in Hut Three with Rose and Calvo-coressi. I liked Telford Taylor and could talk to him as easily about history as about cryptography. He understood, with far more experience behind him than I, that BP housed a very special community. His arrival had been preceded by a visit in July 1942 of two US Navy Reserve lieutenants, R. B. Ely and Joseph J. Eachus, who worked in Hut Eight on Naval Enigma.

Within Hut Six itself we warmly welcomed Captain William Bundy, as he then was, and a group of Americans who joined us in the autumn of 1943. I got to know Bill and his colleagues extremely well. Indeed I was as welcome in their camp at Little Brickhill as if it were my own. An adopted little brown dog still lingers in my mind as a symbol of the informal American military way of life to which I was introduced. I was to keep in touch with many BP Americans after the war. They had been doing the same job in different ranks, as we had. Bundy went on to serve three presidents, Eisenhower, Kennedy and Johnson, and married the daughter of Dean Acheson, Truman's Secretary of State.

Fortunately or unfortunately we could keep no diaries or papers relating to our work at BP so that it is difficult to be sure about vital dates, as an historian must be. Most of the 'military geniuses' who led the West to victory in World War II (there is an agreeable edge to the sub-title of Andrew Roberts's book) did not hesitate to keep them. I myself have two strictly personal diaries of my own for 1943 and for 1944. The first of these was given me by the mother of my best friend at school, an unlikely soldier who had visited Nazi Germany several times before 1939 and became a colonel in the Intelligence Corps. At the end of the Japanese war he was one of the first people to land in what became Indonesia. He died far too young.

My 1943 diary describes very patchily my personal reactions on arriving at BP and more fully my experiences just before arriving there, when I was following a course on cryptography in Bedford. I also have a few papers relating to the course which was concerned entirely with hand cyphers, substitution, transposition and Playfair. For a brief time Bedford figured as prominently in my life as Cambridge had done or as Oxford was to do, for I went on living in 'digs' in Bower Street, Bedford, after I moved to BP and travelled backwards and forwards by train and coach to Bletchley.

I did not move in to the newly built military camp just outside BP in Shenley Road, Bletchley, until January 1944. My diary for 1944 is candid and readable, but while it gives some details of the camp and its characters and of the characters in Hut Six and their personal qualities as I judged them, it gives none about my work.

In this book my Chapter 5, following on after a chapter on BP's huts, particularly Hut Six, deals with the two camps, one the American camp at Little Brickhill, the other best known for its remarkable commandant, Colonel Fillingham of the Durham Light Infantry, for whom it was a matter of intense frustration not to know what Hut Six was. He was never allowed to enter BP. I also write a little about the RAF camp and Woburn Park, home to a sizeable group of Wrens. I had contact there with characters involved in British overseas propaganda. They shared what was in fact a campus.

Fillingham played a bigger part in my Army life than he did in that of Jimmy Thirsk, as I will describe in this volume. Keenly interested in politics, he asked me to join him as 'a real RSM' at the end of the European war when he left Shenley Camp to become head of a Formation College, again near Bedford, that was designed to prepare soldiers for civilian life. Fillingham was no great admirer of Churchill, who visited Hut Six and other parts of BP more than once. Nevertheless, Churchill inspired most of the people working inside BP, and he was to figure prominently in the publicity surrounding its opening up to the public in the 1990s and the first decade of the twenty-first century. A chapter on the Bletchley Park Trust concludes this book. It is not an extra. The story it tells, longer than that of wartime BP, is necessary reading for BPites and visitors to the Park who have no memories of the war.

At the end of the war in 1945 plans were in hand for BP to be closed – the post-war GCHQ moved first to Eastcote in suburban London, which had been an outstation of BP during the war, and then to Cheltenham. The authorities were determined that as few people as possible should know what had been accomplished at BP. Everything no longer needed on the site at BP and its outstations was to be destroyed. We were told that this was on Churchill's personal orders, but it is by no means certain that this was so. The destruction was not total, for two Colossi were to operate elsewhere until the 1960s and some bombes were retained. But it was sad for everyone who stayed on at BP after VE-Day in 1945 to contemplate the loss, particularly for the dedicated people concerned with the Colossus computer at BP, a formidable wartime triumph, to which I will return later in this book.

I believe in retrospect, as, indeed, I did at the time, that whoever gave the orders the scale of such destruction was unnecessary even given a shortage of space. Certainly Churchill himself would never have allowed the Churchill family papers to have been disposed of in such a ruthless manner. I make this judgement knowledgeably, for very soon after the war ended I began helping Churchill, then out of office, with his *History of the English-Speaking Peoples*. It, too, was a team venture, watched over by Colonel William (Bill) Deakin, first Warden of a new Oxford college, St Antony's, founded by a French merchant, Antoine Besse, members of whose families became my close friends. Deakin had been dropped in Yugoslavia during the war to work with Marshal Tito.

It was a coincidental link between us, although I never talked about it to Bill, that at BP the Enigma key which I had to watch over, Puma, was the key employed in Yugoslavia in Luftwaffe messages and that I followed internal conflicts in the Balkans more closely than conflicts in other parts of the world. After the war Bill introduced me to slivovitz, which was the drink served at the opening of St Antony's. The Yugoslav embassy was the first embassy in London at which I was a guest.

It remains sad in retrospect, as it did at the time, that some of the people working at BP who made its success possible received no proper recognition in the form of public honours for their work. It doubtless was thought to be too dangerous to refer in the press to the nature of their contribution towards winning the war, although Winterbotham had been appointed a CBE in 1943 and Nigel de Grey, born in 1886, a CMG in 1945. These were worthy titles. Welchman received only an OBE; it was thoroughly inadequate as an honour at a time when the scrutiny of honours lists rested on more knowledge than it does in the twenty-first century. Hinsley did not receive his knighthood until 1985, long after the Enigma story had become public and it was awarded when his contribution to education was better known than his wartime record.

Milner-Barry joined the Treasury in 1945 with the modest rank of principal, receiving an OBE in 1946, a CBE in 1962 and a KCVO in 1975; this was a natural progression. For everyone else at BP it had to be enough to know that we had served our country. Very few of us became professional code-breakers. We had our own professions, and our lives developed on quite different lines after we had left BP for whatever destination, known or unknown, when the war ended. It was not until 2006 that the Ministry of Defence gave official recognition to BP veterans and out-station veterans.

My chapter in this book on getting into Bletchley is matched by a chapter on getting out of it. Welchman himself, one of ten members of my own college, a remarkable number, who were involved at the very heart of the story, never went back to Sidney Sussex and got out of Bletchley in the most unlikely of ways. Before emigrating to the United States in 1948, which to those who knew him was not in the least surprising, he became director of research for the retail organization the John Lewis Partnership. Hugh Alexander had done this job before the war. Spedan Lewis, chairman of the partnership, wanted Alexander to return to it, but he agreed to return only if Welchman became director of research and he was made assistant director. Alexander stayed in the post for only a very short time, however, from late 1945 to mid-1946.

I must add a word on the title of my book. I have called it *Secret Days*, placing equal emphasis on *Secret* and *Days*. In BP we thought and worked in terms of days, not of years. We never used the term 'the Duration' which figures in my Army Book, now my most invaluable surviving document from the war. Within Hut Six, as in most of BP, each day was divided into three shifts of eight hours. The nights counted therefore: they were incorporated in the days. I deal fully with this in my chapter on Hut Six which draws not only on Welchman but on Calvocoressi, who, from his own perspective, described how next door to us 'we in Hut Three used to get "a bit tetchy" if Hut Six had not broken Red by breakfast time'.

I like the italics placed in sentences in the preface to Hinsley and Stripp's *Codebreakers* referring to a time before I got to BP. 'As early as the end of 1942 BP was reading some four thousand German high-grade signals *a day*, with slightly smaller numbers of Italian and Japanese signals.' I also like Welchman's choice of title 'Today' for Part Four of his first edition of *The Hut Six Story*, although Part Four was omitted from the paperback edition issued in 2001.

Welchman, and John Herivel after him in his book *Herivelismus and the German Military Enigma* (2008), have far more, of course, to say than I do about the basic properties of Enigma, 'the machine' which made it possible for us to succeed in *Breaking the Code*, the title of a brilliant and revealing play by

Hugh Whitemore about Alan Turing, superbly acted by Derek Jacobi. Because of Welchman and Herivel's books I do not intend to go into any detail in my book about the characteristics of the Enigma machine itself. Yet, as Welchman pointed out, and as one of the most recent historians of BP, Hugh Sebag-Montefiore discovered when he wrote his *Enigma: The Battle for the Code* (2000), there are aspects of the Enigma machines – there was not just one –and the German use of them which cannot be left out of any book on Bletchley.

The standard Enigma machines, which the Germans thought to be unbreakable, did not print out encoded messages. As the operating encoder keyed in each letter of clear text into the machine an electrical impulse translated each letter in the message into another letter which lit up on a lampboard of twenty-six small circular windows above the keyboard. Behind the lampboard was a scrambler unit consisting of a fixed wheel at each end with a central space for three rotating wheels (some Kriegsmarine machines had four). The encrypted message was taken down and transmitted in groups of four or five letters. The operating decoder who received the message typed each letter in the message on the keyboard of his own Enigma machine and read the decoded message on his own lampboard. The Enigma machines used at the beginning and end of the process had to be set identically.

Montefiore's was the first British revisionist study of BP, shifting the focus of interpretation of its cryptographic achievements from the skill of code-breakers to the capture of enemy ships and U-boats and the code books and other materials that they were employing. He catches the drama in a series of separate operations, few of which had been so dramatically treated before except by Kahn in his landmark volume *Seizing the Enigma*.

Most previous writers had hinted at the importance of factors other than cryptographic skills, but had dwelt more on the 'carelessness' and the 'errors' of German communications operators. Welchman had focussed on 'wizards'; Sebag-Montefiore focussed on spies, captures at sea, cloak-and-dagger operations and deceptions. Chapter 1 of Sebag-Montefiore's book is called 'The Betrayal', and in it he takes up the remarkable story, told by David Kahn, of how the son of a university history professor, 43-year-old Hans-Thilo Schmidt, then employed in the German Defence Ministry's Cypher Office, walked into the French Embassy in Berlin in June 1931 and handed over vital secret information about the Enigma machine which for personal reasons he wanted to sell to the enemy.

Unlike most later British spies, Schmidt was uninfluenced by political or ideological considerations; he wanted money to live the kind of life he wished for, and continued to provide vital information about Enigma until 1937. By then his brother was a German general. Arrested by the Gestapo in Berlin in March 1943, Hans-Thilo was executed a few months later. Sebag-Montefiore uncovered the family story after tracking down Schmidt's daughter.

Captures of vital documents at sea owed little to spies but were of great importance in enabling BP to break cyphers during the Second World War. Kahn and Sebag-Montefiore gave many details of wartime seizures, the first of them pieces of Enigma hardware sent to BP directly from the German submarine *U-33*, sunk in the Firth of Clyde in February 1940. They both emphasize that the transfer to land of Enigma hardware or codebooks was not a routine process and might well miscarry. Thus, when a boarding party clambered aboard a German trawler, *Krebs*, in Norwegian waters in March 1941, and its leader, Lieutenant

Warmingham, discovered two Enigma wheels, he had never heard of Enigma at all. It was thanks to his enterprise, not to his knowledge, that the Enigma settings for the month were sent on to the naval intelligence section at BP.

One of the most remarkable episodes was taken up later and expanded by Phil Shanahan in his book *The Real Enigma Heroes* (2008). Two British seamen, Able Seaman Colin Grazier and Lieutenant Anthony Fasson, were drowned in the Mediterranean while trying to recover an Enigma machine and new weather codes from a sinking German submarine in October 1942. They acted not only with exceptional courage, posthumously receiving the George Cross, but with equally exceptional presence of mind.

When Shanahan published the story in the *Tamworth Herald* on 27 November 1998, he described it as the story that had the biggest impact in the 160-year old history of the *Herald*. The successful campaign that the *Herald* generated to raise funds for a memorial to Tamworth-born Grazier and Fasson and also to Tommy Brown, canteen assistant, the youngest person to win the George Medal at the age of sixteen, was strongly supported by Robert Harris, author of the novel *Enigma*, and won Phil Shanahan the Freedom of Bletchley Park.

It was in the wake of successes at sea that Churchill had paid his first visit to BP in September 1941, a visit that encouraged a group of leaders in code-breaking in Hut Six and Hut Eight to write to the Prime Minister 'entirely' on 'their own initiative' on 21 October 1941 requesting extra resources for BP itself. Theirs was the most important letter to be sent out of BP during the war. Because of its importance and its implicit criticism of Alastair Denniston, then the operational head of the CG&CS, its authors decided that Stuart Milner-Barry should deliver their letter to Churchill in person at 10 Downing Street. Knowing Milner-Barry later in the war and, indeed, working 'under him', I find their choice of him somewhat difficult to comprehend, unless, as he himself said – and this was probably the reason – he was regarded by them as 'the most expendable member of the quartet'.

Subsequently he has told the remarkable story many times, describing how he took the train from Bletchley to Euston, went to Downing Street, which then – in retrospect, surprisingly – had no barriers in Whitehall, and knocked on the door of Number 10. He got in after saying that he had an important secret and confidential letter to deliver in person to the Prime Minister, but when he was asked for his identity card he could not produce it; he had not taken it with him. Higher officials were then called, and eventually Milner-Barry was assured by a senior officer that the letter would be delivered to Churchill. It was.

The authors of the letter explained that they had not been able to press their case for extra resources through the 'normal channels'. Without them BP could not go on breaking Enigma cyphers. When Churchill read the letter he was stirred to write a minute to Major General Ismay, the highest-ranking military officer attached to him and the Cabinet in Downing Street. 'Make sure [that] they have all they want on extreme priority and report to me that this has been done', and added one of his standard stickers, 'Action This Day'. These words provided the perfect title for the book edited by Ralph Erskine and Michael Smith sixty years later which I acclaimed at the beginning of this chapter.

In this book I will describe more fully what action was taken. In Montefiore's book we encounter a striking coincidence relating to BP. The Victorian-Gothic mansion in Bletchley Park and the estate surrounding it had been the property of Sebag-Montefiore's great, great grandfather, Sir Herbert Leon, a stockbroker who had become a nineteenth-century Liberal MP at a time when W. E.

Gladstone was prime minister. It is also a coincidence that Gladstone's most recent biographer, Roy Jenkins, worked at Bletchley, well out of reach of the Liberal leader's long life. Wartime BP was itself out of reach in time for the clever young television crew who made the lively Channel 4 series of programmes, *Station X* in 1998.

The name Station X itself has an interesting history. The X may sound mysterious, but it refers simply to the placing of the station on a numbered list of radio stations controlled by MI6, the Secret Intelligence Service. The person who was in charge of it and other radio stations for SIS agents was Richard Gambier-Parry, born in 1894, who had been recruited by 'C', the then head of SIS, Admiral Hugh Sinclair, who had acquired the Bletchley Park estate before his death in late 1939. Gambier-Parry installed his section in the old water tower of the mansion at BP. From it he could communicate with established SIS agents scattered through continental Europe. The aerial of the station was placed in the huge sequoia tree which, planted by the Leons, still stands on the lawn in front of the mansion.

Because of lack of adequate space in BP and the visibility from land and air of the radio apparatus installed in the mansion, radio station X was moved to Whaddon Hall, five miles west of Bletchley, in November 1939. This was a more handsome house than the BP mansion, and the station there was built on a height known as Windy Ridge. The Leons had taken an enthusiastic part in the Whaddon Hall hunt. So did Gambier-Parry, who will figure at several points later in this book. So did Hugh Trevor-Roper.

I have regarded it as one of my tasks in the book not only to recall my own Bletchley days but to trace the historiography of BP, and this means going far back before the year 1939. How far back to go is a matter of choice. Michael Smith in his *Station X* looks back to Sir Francis Walsingham, Queen Elizabeth I's spymaster, who set up a decyphering centre in his home in London. He was guided by John Dee, the Queen's astrologer. Christopher Andrew goes back further still in his excellent book *Secret Service* (1985). He starts with Moses: 'In about 1250 BC the Lord instructed Moses to spy out the land of Canaan.' As a consequence, he urged him to secure 'agents' to supply intelligence.

Very quickly, however, Andrew gets out of the Old Testament and after a Victorian Prologue, he lingers, as all historians of cryptography must, in Room 40 in the Admiralty Old Building where at the end of 1914 a permanent staff of five busily at work were providing, in the words of Andrew, 'better intelligence than ever before in British history'. Churchill, an enthusiast for signals intelligence, was First Lord of the Admiralty in the Asquith government between 1911 and 1915; and was fully aware of the historical continuity on 3 September 1939, the day Britain declared war on Germany, when he was back in the same post again. It is not surprising, therefore, that in the first of the 944 letters and telegrams that he sent to President Roosevelt during the Second World War he signed himself 'Former Naval Person'.

Some of the people employed in Room 40 figure prominently in the history of BP during the Second World War. Denniston, recruited to intelligence from Dartmouth, had been at the heart of Room 40, and in 1919 he became head of the newly founded Government Code and Cypher School, a post which he held until February 1942. At least three of his former colleagues in Room 40 joined him at different times in his new organization – Dilly Knox, who had been recruited from King's College in 1915; Nigel de Grey, an Etonian, one of the decrypters of the famous Zimmermann telegram that brought the United States into the First World War; and Frank Birch, a friend of Knox, who was a talented actor as well as a fellow of the same college, King's.

R. V. Jones, as Assistant Director of Intelligence (Science), also started his lively account of intelligence with Churchill, having mentioned briefly Francis Bacon. 'The writings of Winston Churchill are a resplendent source of inspiration, for they scintillate with such phrases as "the gleaming wings of science".' Likewise, Ronald Lewin, who begins his book with the invention of the Enigma machine in 1919, quotes Churchill at the head of his first chapter. For Churchill the Soviet regime was 'a riddle wrapped in a mystery inside an enigma; but perhaps there is a key'.

I start my own account neither with a particular book nor with a particular person but with a particular place, Cambridge, which for long was more famous for its spies of the 1930s than for its cryptographers of the First and Second World Wars. Many of the activities of Anthony Blunt, Guy Burgess, Kim Philby and, the last of them, John Cairncross, who for a time worked at BP, had been exposed more than a decade before Winterbotham published *The Ultra Secret* in 1974. Winterbotham's own autobiography, which appeared in 1989, was called – for wholly laudable reasons – *The Ultra Spy*.

## Chapter 2

# Cambridge

In writing about his years in Hut Six one of my colleagues at BP, the mathematician Derek Taunt, commented *en passant* that had he been either at Marlborough (School) or at Sidney Sussex College, Cambridge, instead of the City of London School and Jesus College, Cambridge, he might just have arrived at BP 'in its great pioneering days' rather than at 'the end of the beginning'. As it was, he arrived there in August 1941.

This was a fair comment as far as Marlborough and Sidney Sussex were concerned, for they both played a quite exceptional part in BP's war effort. Yet Derek, who did not consider Cambridge University as a single entity, or indeed the role of his own college, Jesus, which I know well, was incorrect in implying that 'the great pioneering days' of BP were over when he arrived there in the summer of 1941. There were new challenges ahead even after I arrived at BP two years later, while in the period from January to June 1941, just before Derek arrived, there had been more problems at BP than successes. In 1942 the number of German U-boats increased from under 100 to over 200 and the gross British tonnage lost rose by 80 per cent to 7.85 million. Successful code-breaking depended less on pioneering cryptographic skills than on identifying and exploiting German cryptographic weaknesses and on luck and courage in capturing German code books and other documents at sea.

February 1942 was a cruel month. Denniston had been forced to leave BP when GC&CS was split into two parts – Services at BP and Diplomatic and Commercial (under Denniston) in London. Singapore fell to the Japanese on 15 February, and Churchill felt compelled to reshuffle his Cabinet and bring in the left-wing Sir Stafford Cripps to be leader of the House of Commons. In the same month German Atlantic U-boats stopped using the Hydra cypher, which had first been regularly broken on a continuous basis from August 1941, and BP did not break the new Atlantic U-boat cypher, Triton, until December 1942 when a new short weather code was captured. By then Ultra had played an important though not decisive part in the North African campaign, although it was not until June, July and August 1943 that the German U-boat offensive was finally crippled.

Not even in retrospect was I disappointed that I did not get to BP until the early summer of 1943, when the tide of war was turning, for my pre-BP days in uniform had their distinctive interest. I was glad, however, that I arrived in BP just in time to be welcomed to Hut Six by Welchman. Soon afterwards he left the hut to become ADMech, Assistant Director for Mechanization, working for Travis, who at the start of February 1942 had succeeded Denniston as operational head of the military side of BP. That was a major reorganization.

Like most of the people working in Huts Six and Eight, I do not think that I met 'Jumbo' Travis, as he was known inside the park, more than once or twice, but I continued to see Welchman from time to time before and after he left BP, twice in the United States, to which he moved in 1948. During my two years at BP I was invited several times to his home after he moved to a house in Watling Street, Stony Stratford, where I heard his first wife, Katharine, play the piano and sing. I was glad that Welchman referred to me once in his *The Hut Six Story* when he wrote that 'non-mathematical Sidney men' who joined his team and 'distinguished themselves' at BP were Howard Smith and Asa Briggs. I do not think that Howard, who went on to assume a leading role in post-war diplomacy and intelligence, becoming ambassador to Moscow in 1976 and, controversially, head of MI5 in 1979, would have liked to be described as a non-mathematician.

I used to play bridge against him at Cambridge, partnering the other history scholar at Sidney, John Harrison, who after leaving the college went into the Indian Army, and whose father was a Yorkshire headmaster living near Wentworth Woodhouse, the depot of the Intelligence Corps, which I will describe in my next chapter. Howard was partnered by the senior mathematics scholar, Stephen Betts, who went on from Sidney not to BP but into the Royal Air Force where he became an air commodore. We played so much bridge for a time that we believed we were jeopardizing our degree chances, and, alarmed at the prospect, we dramatically threw the cards away. I quite like having been placed in Welchman's chapter called 'Early Days, December 1939 to 1940' since I did not get to BP from Sidney until more than three years later. Howard was there as a civilian for most of the war.

When I arrived at BP in 1943 it was not from Welchman but from other people working in Hut Six, some of whom I had known in Sidney, Howard more than any other of them, that I learned most about what had been happening at BP since it began to operate in 1939. There was plenty of history in the air as past failures were recalled as well as past successes, and myths were already accumulating about people who worked there, including Turing and Josh Cooper. Gossip preceded myth. It was not days that we talked most of then, as I was learning about what happened between 1939 and 1943, but events. Very quickly I learned, for instance, of the daylight escape of the German battle-cruiser *Gneisenau*, its sister ship *Scharnhorst* and the heavy cruiser *Prinz Eugen* from Brest to Wilhelmshaven on 12 February 1942, an event that shocked Churchill as much as the surrender of Tobruk was to do in June 1942.

In my next chapter I will tell in detail how I got to BP in uniform in June 1943 after a series of moves between 1939 and 1943 that had, as far as I know, nothing to do with Welchman and until 1943 had little to do with code-breaking. In this chapter I want to concentrate on the remarkable part that Cambridge played in the history of BP, and how the playing of that part was related to the parts played by other universities, including Oxford, Edinburgh and Glasgow, and other institutions, not all of them universities. Notable among the latter was the Post Office Research Establishment in Dollis Hill in north-west London. In general, I conclude that BP had less in common with a university than has often been suggested. At the time one of the two key Cambridge figures, Welchman, probably thought the same. Although Sidney Sussex continued to pay his fellowship stipend throughout the war I do not think that he often went back to the college during the war, and as I have mentioned he did not return to Cambridge when the war ended.

Nevertheless, until C. P. Snow, fellow of Christ's College, Cambridge, took over the recruiting of scientists for the war effort in May 1941, Welchman did much of the recruiting for Hut Six himself, never confining his attention to Sidney Sussex or to Cambridge. He later described his efforts as 'pirating'. He recruited women as well as men. One of them, Ione Jay, was a girl at a school where Welchman's father, a canon of the Church of England, was chairman of the governors. Gordon Welchman visited the school in February 1941 and suggested that Ione should join a secret .

'Government communications organization under the Foreign Office'. On 19 April she found herself at BP and stayed there until July 1945.

Ione had no experience of Cambridge nor was she a mathematician, but it was through such personal links that BP was constituted. A large proportion of the people recruited were of university age. Cambridge itself was not a monolithic university, and Welchman's first recruit, the mathematician Dennis Babbage (not a descendant of Charles Babbage), came from Magdalene College, smaller than the Jesus College to which Taunt belonged. I got to know Babbage well at BP, as I had known Magdalene as an undergraduate when I listened to Bennett lecturing.

Each college in Cambridge had its own culture. The college with which BP is usually linked is King's, often contrasted with Trinity, where Welchman had been a mathematics scholar from 1925 to 1928 before becoming a mathematics lecturer and later, in 1931, a fellow of Sidney Sussex. The two leading King's figures at BP, whom I have already introduced, contrast sharply with Welchman and each other: Alan Turing was born in 1912 and Dilly Knox in 1884.

Knox, who was the son of an Anglican clergyman who became bishop of Manchester, had arrived in King's from Eton as early as 1903. He was one of four equally memorable brothers described by his niece, Penelope Fitzgerald, in a scholarly family memoir of 1977, *The Knox Brothers*, published in a year when some, but not all, of the secret papers relating to BP in the Public Record Office had recently been opened up. Dilly's eldest brother became editor of *Punch*, another brother was an Anglican monk, and his youngest brother, a Roman Catholic priest, was a great recruiter for his own faith. For his niece Dilly was the 'very epitome of an absent-minded professor': he even forgot to invite two of his three brothers to his wedding.

Turing, who at the beginning of his BP life worked with Dilly, was the son of an Indian civil servant, and had arrived in King's in 1931 from Sherborne, Dorset, a school as different from Welchman's Marlborough as King's College was from Trinity College. Turing had tried to get a scholarship to Trinity first, and his school had approached Pembroke College too, which ten years later was to be the Cambridge college with the largest number of left-wing undergraduates. There was to be more revolutionary talk there then than in Trinity.

Knox and Turing were men around whom legends cluster. Turing was an acknowledged mathematical genius, although Sherborne had not thought him as such, who went back often to King's College during the war, and, indeed, after the war, to read and to think. Before the war he had carried out fundamental mathematical research on the other side of the Atlantic, and after the war ended he moved to a new mathematics division in the National Physical Laboratory at Bushy Park and, after two frustrating years and a brief return to King's, in 1948 to the Manchester Computing Laboratory. A Manchester neuro-surgeon who met him then for the first time felt that 'he was so unversed in worldly ways, so childlike' that he had 'never quite grown up'.

Sadly Turing did not grow old. His life ended tragically when, having been persecuted as a homosexual, he committed suicide by taking cyanide. There is now a statue of Turing in Manchester, sculpted in bronze by Glyn Hughes and located on the city's Gay Heritage Trail. It was erected in 2001 and unveiled on his birthday, 23 June. There are other statues too. Turing has also inspired the longest and fullest biography of anyone who worked at BP, Andrew Hodges's *Alan Turing: An Enigma of Intelligence* (1983).

Welchman, six years older than Turing, has inspired no biography. Yet it was Welchman, working at first with Tony

Kendrick, recruited by Dilly Knox, who more than Knox or Turing made BP what it was, a flexible institution capable of adaptation and development which lacked any formal diagram of its organization structure until 1944. An earlier effort to produce one was marked 'MOST SECRET Most Misleading and Most Inaccurate'. That was dated September 1943, the month that Welchman left Hut Six and became Assistant Director, Mechanization, under Commander Travis, who was neither a cryptographer nor a Cambridge man but had worked in GC&CS before the war. He had advised the government on what types of codes and cyphers should be in use in Britain.

Travis's senior military colleague at BP, Colonel J. H. Tiltman, seven years younger and a brilliant cryptographer, 'a giant among cryptographers', gave him effective backing. Tiltman knew everything that was going on in BP, both on the German and the Japanese sides, and he influenced all aspects of organization and policy. He was promoted to the rank of brigadier in March 1944. Travis was knighted the same year.

Derek Taunt, whom I quoted at the beginning of this chapter, was right to refer not only to the personal role of Welchman – and of Marlborough – in BP history but to the role of Sidney Sussex College, a college of which I became a scholar in 1938. When war was declared in 1939 it was a college very different in its size, its social composition and its culture from King's. I have found in my own archives an interesting letter of 1 November 1939 written by the then Master of Sidney Sussex, G. A. Weekes, to a recent graduate, who never then or thereafter had anything to do with BP, who asked him what was happening to the college under the impact of war. The Master informed him that Welchman, along with his and my history tutor E. J. (Jim) Passant, had 'left for the

Captain Ridley's famous shooting party which examined BP as a wartime intelligence site in 1938, recommending Sinclair to acquire it.

Before I was called up in 1942 I was expecting to work in radar; like other historians I thought I was going to be converted into a scientist but since there proved to be enough scientists I became a signalman instead.

A page from the German Enigma users' manual.

Enigma machines in use. *Below left*, a three-rotor version in the famous photo of General Heinz Guderian's command vehicle in France in 1940; and *below* a four-rotor machine in the cramped confines of a U-boat.

*Left to right:* Alistair Denniston, first head of GC&CS; Professor E. R. P. Vincent, an Italian specialist who worked in Hut Four; and Colonel John Tiltman, who achieved important breaks in both German and Japanese cyphers and after the war worked for the American National Security Agency.

Commander Edward 'Jumbo' Travis, who took over from Denniston as operational head of BP in 1942. Welchman described him as being of the 'bulldog breed'.

The iconic BP figure Alan Turing. He has been described as the creator of the modern digital age.

Poznań University's Mathematics Institute where many of Poland's future cryptographers studied before the war. The photo was taken in 1939 with German soldiers in the crowd outside.

Leaders of the Polish–French Bruno team in October 1939, Lt Col Gwido Langer (*left*), Maj Gustave Bertrand (*centre*), and their British liaison officer Capt Kenneth Macfarlan.

Marian Rejewski, one of the small team of Polish mathematicians who broke Enigma.

Rejewski's colleagues Henryk Zygalski and Jerzy Różycki in unoccupied southern France in 1940–1.

A group of code-breakers watch a BP rounders game. Alistair Denniston is standing at right, while fifth from left is George McVittie, head of weather cryptanalysis.

Gordon Welchman, who devised the Hut system at BP. He later told the *Hut Six Story* in a memorable book which alarmed the authorities.

Dilly Knox, a genuine eccentric. J. M. Keynes, an old friend from his Eton days, described Knox as being 'sceptical of most things except those that chiefly matter, that is affection and reason'.

Myself when young. I had reached the Intelligence Corps and BP and could now wear a peaked cap rather than a forage cap.

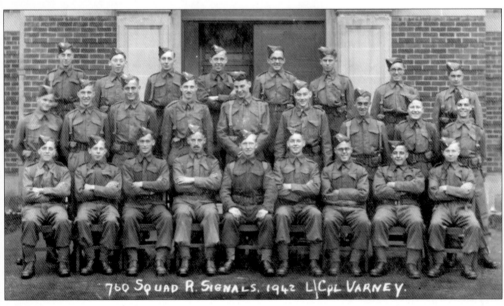

760 SQUAD R. SIGNALS. 1942 L\CPL VARNEY.

My first signals platoon at Catterick camp in 1942. The fifth from the left in the top row was a brilliant boogie-woogie player; the one on the extreme right in the front row was my main opponent at ping-pong. It was a very happy platoon.

Little Brickhill. With me is the historian who taught me almost everything I know about the American Civil War, LeRoy Fisher, from Oklahoma. I had never heard of Oklahoma in 1939.

Three friends from Hut Six on a day out not far from Bletchley. Since I took the picture I presume the almost empty glass on the table was mine.

Major Ralph Tester, twenty years older than me, a pioneer cryptologist. Before and after the war he worked for Unilever.

Donald Michie, born in Rangoon, was one of the outstanding people in BP, which he joined soon after leaving school.

William Tutte, born in 1917, the son of an estate gardener in Newmarket, was not only a hero of BP but a hero of self-help.

Max Newman. In 1945 his section at BP, the Newmanry, employed 20 cryptanalysts, 6 engineers and 273 Wrens.

Foreign Office', the destination with which Passant, though never Welchman, was always to be identified.

Another fellow, J. A. Ratcliffe, had left the college too for 'special service under the Air Ministry', and, Passant's colleague, a young history tutor, R. C. Smail, an authority on crusader castles, had joined the Army and was a 2nd lieutenant. 'We have [thus] parted with a larger proportion of our teaching staff', Weekes added, 'than any other College.' Smail's movements were known, but 'we are not told', the Master went on, 'where Passant, Welchman or Ratcliffe now are.' With his long memory the Master concluded that 'the aspect of Cambridge is very different from what it was in 1914'. He did not explain why, but he headed his letter with a PS at the top, 'If there is the remotest chance of this falling into enemy hands, perhaps you will burn it when read.' It was not burnt. The recipient later gave it to me.

The main record of those Sidney undergraduates who left Cambridge for BP not in one single burst but in a sequence, ending with a brilliant young historian, Paul Coles, is to be found not in the college records, but in the National Archives. My friend Peter Lipscombe, until recently honorary chairman of the Sidney Sussex Society, who has helped me immensely in examining both these archive collections, has described the ten Sidney students who went to BP at various times during the war as 'Sidney's Secret Service'. 'These extraordinary men not only were outstanding in their own field, but each had the ability to "think outside the box" or have that flash of inspiration which is essential to the greatest breakthroughs.'

The first of Welchman's pupils to arrive were David Rees and Howard Smith in December 1939, with John Herivel and Malcolm Chamberlain arriving in January 1940. They were founder members of Welchman's Machine Room, which was

directly concerned with code-breaking, side by side with the
Registration Room and Intercept Room, the names of which
speak for themselves. Herivel, who sadly died in the month when
I was completing this book, is, as I have mentioned, the only one
to have written his own personal account of his Bletchley days,
*Herivelismus*, which, like Hugh Sebag-Montefiore's book, starts
with the Enigma machine and goes on to explain the unique contribution that he, Herivel, made to the breaking of the Luftwaffe
Enigma cyphers.

It is a good story. Brooding over the embers of a fire in his
Bletchley billet, he imagined a way that German operators might
take short cuts in their handling of Enigma encyphering and use
indicators close to the official Enigma ring setting of the day. If
this were so the number of decode variables needed to find the
ring setting would be dramatically reduced.

It was Kendrick who invented the word Herivelismus, one of
the *isms* proclaimed in BP. Leslie Yoxall, older than any of the
arrivals from Sidney Sussex, is also associated with an *ismus*,
'Yoxallismus', an approach to the recovery of the plugging of naval
keys. He is mentioned neither by Welchman nor by Herivel, but
should be singled out for the special contribution he made to the
breaking of Naval Enigma. There was a third *ismus*, Banburismus,
without which it would have been almost impossible to break the
Dolphin cypher regularly.

I was aware before I went to BP that Smith was not in the same
class among Sidney's mathematicians as Herivel or Rees, the latter
becoming a Fellow of the Royal Society and Professor of Mathematics at Exeter University after the war. Yet Herivel would have
liked to be an historian not a mathematician and Rees was not
only a good mathematician but always got his historical facts
right. Welchman, though himself a competent historian, capable

of separating out different phases of BP's history, sometimes got his facts and dates wrong. Critical of Hinsley's mistakes, most of which Hinsley acknowledged, he himself called Chamberlain John, not Malcolm, and suggested that I was at BP long before I was.

Overshadowing all this he was wise enough from the start to appreciate that there was a place for non-mathematicians at BP, and the first person that he signed on was Stuart Milner-Barry, whom he had got to know while Milner-Barry was studying classics at Trinity College and Welchman was studying mathematics. After going down Milner-Barry lived in Cambridge, where his sister was an academic and could suggest names of suitable women for BP.

In the future many of these were to come from Scotland and there was an important link with Scotland almost from the start of the war. One of the early recruits to BP, Alexander Craig Aitken, entered BP as a Foreign Office civilian in 1940. He was a lecturer in mathematics at Edinburgh University, and because of his age and reputation he was always known inside Hut Six as Dr Aitken. (In the admirable index to Welchman's *The Hut Six Story* he is simply 'Mr Aitken'.) He had no Cambridge connection, but again there were to be ripple effects. Some of the women recruits from Scotland were university graduates and mathematicians, others were linguists. They came not only from Edinburgh University but from Glasgow, St Andrews and Aberdeen. In my view the part that they played in Hut six has never been given adequate attention.

One veteran cryptographer at BP, Hugh Foss, was well known to me because of his striking appearance – red hair, red beard and sandals. Not the least of his accomplishments was that, like Oliver Lawn, he was a passionate performer of Scottish dancing. Foss had been a schoolboy at Marlborough and an undergraduate at Christ's College, Cambridge, before joining GC&CS five years before Nigel de Grey, a veteran of Room 40. One of Foss's early tasks had been to examine an Enigma machine in 1927; it was then being used commercially (although its design differed somewhat from the wartime versions). Born in Kobe, Japan, Foss switched from naval Enigma in Hut Eight to Japanese naval cyphers after the beginning of the Japanese war. Since childhood he had been fluent in Japanese and it seemed natural that he should be transferred to Washington as an officer handling Japanese cyphers. He stayed on in GCHQ until his retirement in 1953.

By 1953 relationships had changed far more than names, as Richard J. Aldrich has shown in his *GCHQ: The Uncensored* [a word far more acceptable to me than authorized] *Story of Britain's Most Secret Intelligence Agency* (2010), the first chapter of which is called 'Bletchley Park and Beyond'. One aspect of change, reflecting the transition from war to peace, was the relationship between code-breakers, college dons and schoolmasters. As Foss's record shows, Marlborough before the war, mainly through its mathematics, had a close connection as a school with BP and GC&CS, noted by Derek Taunt, even if it was not quite as close a connection as that between Eton and King's. Indeed Marlborough made as distinctive a contribution to the life of Hut Six as Sidney Sussex did.

Welchman, who, as we have seen, was associated with both, went to Marlborough as a schoolboy in 1920 where he was taught by an outstanding mathematics master, A. Robson, with whom he kept in touch after leaving school, collaborating with him in producing mathematics textbooks. When he moved to BP he appealed to Robson for help in providing recruits, some of whom had become mathematics teachers in other schools.

Outstanding amongst these was John Manisty, who after the war was to leave his mark on Winchester – he became known as 'the genius of Winchester' – but even the outlines of his BP career were unknown to his pupils and colleagues,. I worked under John at BP and went to visit him at Winchester several times after the war. He would never have used the word 'under', and he had all the right personal qualities to persuade BP's civilians and service personnel to feel that they were part of a team, using first names and avoiding all references to rank. As head of the watch in Hut Six under Milner-Barry he maintained effective cooperation with Hut Three where there were probably more eccentric characters than there were in Hut Six, some of them old and far more difficult than my immediate colleagues in Hut Six. Some of the latter were younger than I was.

Among the very young recruits who came to the watch direct from Marlborough before they went on to university were Arthur Read and Bob Roseveare, who took up his scholarship at Cambridge after the war at the age of twenty-two, reading not medicine, as he had planned to do in 1942, but mathematics. Following in Welchman's footsteps, after Cambridge he joined the John Lewis organization before moving out to South Africa. Among the other bright public school boys at BP was Nigel Forward, in my view, then and now, the brightest of them all. I lost touch with him completely after the war, but I later learned that he served as a private secretary to a sequence of prime ministers.

In a period of rapid expansion Stuart Milner-Barry, Welchman's successor, was sensitive to the dangers of losing the harmonious relations which he had inherited. He had already paid careful attention to recruitment before he took over what he himself never called management. ('Administration' was always the BP word, as it was in the Civil Service.) One of his most able recruits, a lawyer, John Monroe, came from the Army. Known as JG to distinguish him from Manisty, JC, JG had a sister who was known to Milner-Barry, and it was Milner-Barry who arranged for him to be interviewed by Welchman and Tiltman.

He was allowed to be released from his current post to pursue his military service at BP. Such a straightforward move would have been impossible a few months later when the rules of recruitment were formalized. It then became impossible, because of the increased volume of work in Hut Six, to release 'other ranks' to go off to officer training and return to BP with commissions. It was left to Tiltman, not Welchman or Milner-Barry, to deal with the implications of this, and fortunately he was as wise a counsellor as he was a brilliant cryptographer.

Welchman himself had not escaped the complications of military service rules as applied to BP cryptographers. When he moved to BP in 1939 he had been designated a temporary civil servant in a branch of the Foreign Office, but when his age group was called up he received a notice telling him to report to a unit of the Royal Artillery in the north of England. He showed the notice to the Foreign Office administrators at BP, who said that they would deal with the matter. They did not, nor did they when he received a second order from the colonel of the Royal Artillery unit. As a farcical result the Chief Constable of Buckinghamshire, by a coincidence a relative of his wife, told him that he had received a warrant for his arrest.

At last the Foreign Office intervened successfully, but Welchman was now told that in order to be discharged from his military service he first would have to enlist! And so he did, travelling to a small Royal Artillery establishment near to BP which was staffed by an Army sergeant. More farce followed. Welchman filled in a 'few forms' and the sergeant congratulated him on becoming a gunner and told him to return the next day after medical examination. The doctor who would have carried it out that day, he said, was out at lunch. Welchman succeeded in finding him and tried to report the result of the examination to the sergeant, finding that he in turn was now out at lunch. Once again Welchman found the missing person, and was duly discharged. He had been in the Army for twenty minutes. Welchman ended the writing of the main part of *The Hut Six Story* in what he called this 'light vein'.

The story of Harold Fletcher, which Welchman also told, had a serious as well as a light side to it. A school and university friend of Welchman, Fletcher, a senior manager working in a reserved occupation, was asked by Welchman to join him at BP early in 1940. He replied that his firm would only release staff if they joined the armed forces, and so he did, being placed as a private in the Intelligence Corps. For eight months he was in uniform, being promoted to lance corporal. Travis tried for the next six months to find a suitable military unit to which Fletcher could be attached as an officer, but had no luck. At that point, however, Fletcher's business firm changed its rules, allowing him to be demobilized, placed on the special reserve, and employed for wartime duties by the Foreign Office. He remained in charge of the important section at BP concerned with liaison with the British Tabulating Machines (BTM) company, which was manufacturing bombes for BP at Letchworth. His strength was that he was a real manager, not an administrator.

# Chapter 3

# Getting Inside BP

How I got to Cambridge from Keighley, an industrial town, later to become part of Bradford, in what was then the West Riding of Yorkshire, is in some respects more interesting than how I got from Cambridge to BP, and since the two narratives are connected – and not just through Gordon Welchman – I must explain the connection between them.

Keighley was no less an unlikely point of departure than Wyke, a smaller township to the south of Bradford from which Major Edward Rushworth of Hut Three came – I knew him well at BP – or indeed than the distant city of Rangoon in Burma where Donald Michie was born. The great city of Smyrna in Asia Minor in which George McVittie, head of the BP section cracking weather codes, was born was an unusual starting point for many of his later journeys. After the war he taught mathematics at King's College, London, where one of his pupils was the writer of science fiction, Arthur C. Clarke. McVittie subsequently crossed the Atlantic to the University of Illinois, where he worked in radio astronomy, building a radio telescope. In 1958 his colleagues published in *Nature* some of the earliest orbital data relating to *Sputnik I*.

My headmaster at Keighley Boys' Grammar School, an old grammar school founded in the late seventeenth century, was a devoted Sidney Sussex man, Neville Hind, who had read history at the college. His own experience focussed and sharpened all the advice that he gave to me. 'Read history, not English', which was the subject at which I then excelled. 'Go to Cambridge, not to Oxford.' 'Do not go to St John's but to Sidney Sussex.' Had he not been so firm I might well have gone to St John's, the college to which Hinsley won a scholarship from Queen Mary's Grammar School in Walsall in 1937, the same year as I won mine to Sidney Sussex. Students at Keighley Grammar School who wanted to read mathematics or science were always advised to try first for St John's.

No member of my family had ever been at a university before, and my father, who had been a victim of the great depression in the 1930s, which hit my family particularly hard, needed per-suading by my headmaster to make him place education first in thinking about my future. I knew no more of Cambridge colleges than my father did and nothing of public schools except what I read about them in boys' magazines, like the *Magnet*. I had never heard of Marlborough, but I knew vaguely of Eton, and I had listened to John Snagge's running commentaries on the Boat Race. I was clearest about what I did not want to do. I did not want to stay in Keighley, although I loved the town and belonged there. In my own more positive thinking about my future I had vague ideas of becoming a newspaper editor without knowing much more about editors than about dons. Nor did I clearly distinguish between journalists and editors.

As far as my immediate future was concerned, I knew that if I were to continue my education I did not want to go to Leeds University. Studying at a local university was not then believed to be a good idea. You had to get away. McVittie, whom I have mentioned, had connections with Leeds University: for a time he was a lecturer there, and he married the daughter of a Leeds professor of education, John Strong. In Leicester the future historian Jack Plumb, who was to work in Hut Three in BP, was more determined to get out of his city than I was. While working on a Kriegsmarine hand cypher, he was billeted with Anthony de Rothschild at Ascott House, Wing. This was the best of all BP billets.

James Passant, my history supervisor at Sidney Sussex, to which I duly applied, had also supervised Neville Hind. Passant was born in 1891, the same year as my father, and had become a fellow of the college in 1919 just after the end of the First World War. He stayed on as a fellow, with the Second World War as a break, until 1946 when he became Director of Research and Librarian and Keeper of the Papers at the Foreign Office. That was a post directly concerned with intelligence. He sat on wartime committees with representatives of BP and was attached to BP until 1941.

Neville Hind and Jim (or James as I first knew him) are the two men who have most shaped my life. Neville knew nothing of what I did at BP, Passant knew everything that he cared to know about BP and its far from straightforward relationships with other agencies dealing with intelligence, a word which I never heard him use. He joined Welchman at BP very early in the war and often stayed in wartime Bletchley. His role in my own life was in some way 'paternal' in a fashion that Neville's never was. When I went up to Sidney in December 1937 to try for a scholarship it was Jim who interviewed me. Having read my papers, which included a long essay on the abdication of Edward VIII the previous year (I cannot remember what I wrote about it), he told me at my interview, 'You are only a baby, Briggs, but I am going to give you a scholarship, because there is going to be a war, and I would like you to have time to take your degree before you go into the forces.'

I was young enough for this to be possible, and I regularly took note of his accompanying advice to improve my German. Neville helpfully arranged for me to have one-to-one lessons from the school's German mistress. I also on my own initiative took private lessons in Italian, which I paid for, just how I cannot recall. My teacher was a Czech lady who got out of Prague before Munich. During the war I might well have been involved with Italian, not German, either at BP or in Woburn Park.

I had one shock in December 1937 just after I got back from my first trip to Cambridge. The letter from Sidney Sussex telling me that I had got a major scholarship was unaccountably delayed over a long weekend, and before I received it I knew the names of all the other boys from my school who had secured Cambridge scholarships and exhibitions in other colleges, including the head prefect who had got a science scholarship at St John's. I was in despair when, remembering what Passant had told me, I went to school on the following Monday morning having still heard nothing. Happily for me despair turned into delight when – and it was a unique occasion – I was called by the senior master, a chemist nicknamed 'Fatty Acid', to leave the platform on which the prefects sat together with the masters at Assembly and go out into the corridor and see the headmaster before he came into the hall to conduct it. 'You have got a senior scholarship', Neville told me simply, and, as happy as I was, we went into the hall together. That in retrospect – and only in retrospect – was the first lead-in to my life in BP.

As I was beginning this chapter I read of the death of Alan Stripp, who has been one of the liveliest historians of BP and whose account of how he got into BP from Cambridge, very directly, was quite different from my own. His father was a mathematics teacher, and he was reading history in Trinity College when, in the spring of 1943, just before I reached BP, now in uniform, his college tutor sent him a note telling him about the impending visit of an officer who was interviewing undergraduates to take up specialized but unspecified war work. Stripp applied to be interviewed, and after being asked about chess, crossword puzzles and musical scores, was informed almost at once that he was to start a course not in cryptography but in Japanese at Bedford. His tutor was George Kitson Clark, an historian of the nineteenth century whose lectures I attended in Cambridge and who became a friend of mine after the war. He came from a Leeds industrial family.

In his book *Codebreaker in the Far East* (1989) Stripp begins his first chapter 'Cambridge, Bedford and Yorkshire' with the general question 'How do people become code-breakers?' It is a question which I am often asked and which is relevant to any analytical study of the war effort. Stripp's experiences of code-breaking began later than mine, followed a different order and took him to different places. I start my book as a boy in Yorkshire; he started his as an undergraduate in Cambridge, where he was reading history several years after me. After finishing his Japanese course he was commissioned and sent to the depot of the Intelligence Corps at Wentworth Woodhouse, near Rotherham in Yorkshire.

I had taken part as a private in the Intelligence Corps in the move of the depot, called 'Other Ranks Wing', to Wentworth Woodhouse from King Alfred's College, Winchester in 1942. It was a secret move – we did not know where we were going – but after what seemed an endless journey north we were greeted by a brass band at Rotherham station. There were no brass bands for Alan. Yet, unlike me, he knew where he was going, and he was going to Wentworth as a young officer, I as a simple signalman. Once in Wentworth, however, our experiences were much the same. I have never written about mine but he describes devastatingly the archaic regime which horrified him as it horrified me.

Wentworth Woodhouse was one of England's great houses. We were in the stables. There was an immense gap between officers (commanded by an aristocrat, more distant than any Earl Fitzwilliam ever had been, with an adjutant beside him who fully deserved his nickname 'The Blond Brute') and men, all of whom were far more intelligent than the officers were. The non-commissioned officers were mostly discarded Guardsmen, who went out of their way to bully some of the cleverest men in the country whom they thoroughly despised. Their only skill was in catching people out. The relationship between intelligence, with a small i and Intelligence with a large one was never really sorted out during the war. There was a multiplicity not only of agents but of agencies.

After passing through Wentworth Woodhouse, Stripp was posted to India to break Japanese codes at the Wireless Experimental Centre (WEC), not far from New Delhi, sometimes described wrongly as India's BP. I went on, uncommissioned, to pursue a Field Security course run on very different lines from Wentworth Woodhouse at Matlock. Years later, as I have noted, Stripp was to edit along with Hinsley *Codebreakers: The Inside Story of Bletchley Park*, an indispensable source for the historian of BP, and he also wrote a novel *The Code Snatch*. After returning from India after the war he had gone back to Trinity College in order to complete his studies. Subsequently he went on to join the British Council in Portugal, where a close girlfriend of mine at BP also went.

I do not remember Stripp from BP, but I remember clearly my own Cambridge days long before his. The university was beautifully quiet, but my days were never dull. It was not easy to concentrate on medieval history after the war in the west began and France collapsed. I was never taught history by Passant, for he was already getting caught up in his intelligence duties. I knew nothing about them, and it was only years later that I learned that at the beginning of the war, while I was still in Cambridge, he had often stayed in Bletchley. When he was at home, quite effortlessly he made me feel like a member of his wonderful family. He did the same for several of my contemporaries. At family parties we dressed up and played games together with his wife and two daughters. They became friends.

Audrey, his wife, I saw regularly after Jim died: she moved to the Oxford area after I became a fellow of Worcester College in 1945. The Passants' younger daughter married an Oxford friend who was a post-war president of the Union. The older daughter had married a Cambridge, later LSE, psychologist, Norman Hotopf, who devised intelligence tests for army officers. He tried his first test out on his father-in-law who got a very low score. One of the qualifications for code-breaking was psychological, the ability to get inside another mind. There were very few professional psychologists at BP, but in their absence historians had to be psychologists all the time.

The only psychologist I knew at BP, Wing Commander Oscar Oeser, future professor of psychology at Melbourne University, was uninterested in intelligence tests, but played an important part in Hut Three, the intelligence hut. He ran a small unit, 3L, which assessed the day's traffic and established priorities. He was a key member of a TICOM team at the end of the war.

During the war I was found, in Passant's absence, a great tutor, Ernest Barker, who had just retired from the professorship of political science. He was a scholar with a foothold in Cambridge, Oxford and London universities, and I worked enthusiastically with him both on medieval and modern history. His northern accent, carefully cultivated, was far stronger than mine, and his knowledge of German political theory led me to German books that I would never otherwise have read. At the height of the invasion scare of 1940 he sent a postcard to my home address in Keighley that was written entirely in German, and, although an internal postal item, it was passed over to the censor before being sent on to me. It dealt with an obscure German political theorist of whom Hitler had probably never heard.

The incident, evoking many half-forgotten memories of war, reminds me in retrospect of an incident concerning an exceptionally clever history contemporary of mine at Cambridge, Hrothgar Habakkuk, from Barry in Wales who spent part of the war in BP. While, as a postgraduate, he was examining a batch of medieval maps and records in a Cambridgeshire barn, he was disturbed by a policeman who asked him his name. When he replied Habakkuk he had to spell it out, and when he was then asked what was his first name and replied Hrothgar, the policeman took him along to the police station for further questioning. Hugh Trevor-Roper was to have a somewhat similar experience in 1940. Strolling through the Cornish countryside and looking, as he admitted, scruffy in his unbuttoned uniform, he was arrested by the Home Guard on suspicion of being a spy.

I cannot remember meeting Habakkuk at BP, but I do remember meeting another young historian from Cambridge, like Habakkuk slightly older than I was, Peter Laslett, who had a fascinating post-war career ahead of him at Trinity College, a career which criss-crossed with mine. We were used to talking about BBC politics and continuing education before he and a team he inspired turned to family history. His book *The World We Have Lost* (second edition, 1971) became a classic. We never talked about BP until the 1980s, when we both knew, drawing on the title of his book, that Bletchley was a world that was totally lost to us except through our memories – and through the first books about it that we were reading. There were few memorabilia. These were to be collected much later.

In recalling my undergraduate years in Cambridge, I always pay the warmest tribute that I can to the pre-war state scholarship scheme, which I am sure should have been retained long after the war in the national interest. It was not restricted to particular subjects. One of the men I would most like to have met at BP, but never did, benefitted from the scheme even more than I. Without any Neville Hind to guide him, William Thomas (Bill) Tutte, born in 1917, four years before me, the son of a gardener working at the Rutland Arms Hotel in Cheveley near Newmarket, won a state scholarship and a college scholarship at Trinity in 1935. He was then a pupil at the Cambridge and County High School, and at Trinity he read natural sciences, specializing in chemistry. He got a first-class degree in chemistry and was a treasured member of the Trinity Mathematics Society.

Having been called up for national service in 1940, Tutte made his way quickly to BP in January 1941, where he made an important personal contribution to the solving of high-grade secret communications from Hitler to his generals or between Berlin and army groups. The Tunny machine (from the Fish group) was to figure almost as prominently as Enigma in the history of BP, and related also to the development of the Colossus computer. When these messages were read in 1944 intelligence 'of crucial importance' was secured, as Hinsley described it, 'on Germany's appreciations of the Allied invasion intentions and on its own plans for countering them'.

After the war Tutte returned to Cambridge and secured a doctorate in mathematics and in 1948 moved to Canada. He proved that it is possible to change academic course as well as academic location. Likewise, before I had any idea of going to BP, in my last year as an undergraduate at Sidney Sussex in 1940–1, a determined effort was made by the physics fellow in my own college, John Ratcliffe, to draw me from history into science after I had taken my Part II examination in the summer. (Passant had secured his wish and I was still below call-up age.) It was essential to the success of Ratcliffe's plan for me that I should be deemed suitable by C. P. Snow, fellow at Christ's College, who in the spring of 1941 had just been given the task of choosing which of the 'best brains in the country' should be employed on the science side of the war effort, including choices for Welchman's Hut Six at BP. When he wrote his book *The Hut Six Story* Welchman did not know whether in 1941 Snow knew what work Hut Six was carrying out at BP. I am not sure myself whether Ratcliffe knew what Welchman was doing either.

Unfortunately I kept no note of my interview with Snow, but I still remember it vividly. When I walked into what seemed to me his very gloomy college room Snow struck me – first impressions – as being the ugliest man I had ever seen. Fortunately I knew nothing about him then. Had I known anything I would have been intimidated. Subsequently I was to read all Snow's novels, and learned that by a strange coincidence the original title of one of them was *Passant*. I got to know Snow's wife, Pamela Hansford Johnson, a little – she also was a novelist – and I reviewed his controversy with F. R. Leavis on science and culture in the *Scientific American*. (Jim Passant's old college, Downing, was the Cambridge college which Leavis placed on the map.)

Back in 1941, I found Snow pleasant and supportive, and I answered all his questions to his satisfaction. I was duly approved for radar service which I then knew rather more about than cryptography. I was told that in due course – no specific time was mentioned – I would be informed when and where to report. I knew of the Telecommunications Research Establishment at Malvern before I knew of BP, and I subsequently got to know A. P. Rowe, then its head, with whom I talked about science and universities. In a future world of student fees, which neither of us could foresee – nor could Snow – I would probably have been required to study science at university, not history.

When I left Cambridge in the early summer of 1941 I felt that I would be moving to a radar centre very soon, but in the meantime I returned to Keighley. I had had to keep secret my plan of taking a London University external BSc(Econ.) examination in my college in parallel to the historical Tripos or the master and senior tutor would have refused to allow me to take it. Before I ever signed the Official Secrets Act I had, therefore, learnt how to keep secrets.

I did not have to keep this secret for long. To my immense surprise, a few days before the London results were published, I had a telephone call from Harold Laski, Professor of Politics at the LSE, asking me why I had not applied for the Gerstenberg Studentship, a coveted research fellowship, based on my performance in the BSc(Econ.) examination. I wrote back to him that I had not applied because I knew nothing about the studentship, but added that I would now apply. I duly got the studentship and expected that it would be to LSE that I would go after the war ended. It made no difference to my wartime plans. The fact that I got the studentship made it possible for me to inform the master and senior tutor at Sidney Sussex with impunity, and they then seemed as happy as I was.

Motivations are curious, as I came to appreciate more fully between leaving Cambridge and reaching BP in 1943. Although I had personal reasons for taking the London examination in parallel with the historical Tripos these were not my only motives in the summer of 1941. As well as the desire to supplement my knowledge of history, an empirical study, with the study of a subject that demanded abstract analysis (I used this language), I concluded from the experience that it would not be unrealistic for me to contemplate becoming a wartime scientist. I had not then heard the word boffin but I was all too familiar with the word pundit.

There was a curious hiatus in my life, however, from 1941 to 1942 with Neville Hind once more coming to my aid. After going down from Cambridge I heard nothing further about going off to join Ratcliffe in radar, and all my enquiries, including enquiries to Snow, produced only the answer 'Wait'. I could not live on nothing and I decided, therefore, to live at home in Keighley and take up war-supply teaching. My degree was an adequate qualification for doing so, and I chose in the first instance a big secondary modern school in Keighley, Highfield, which had a delightful and sophisticated headmaster, whose daughter was a London actress, and who was far more interesting to talk to than Neville. I learned an immense amount from this experience, but I became increasingly worried about my not being allowed to do something directly for the war effort. My talents were not being put to use. I was also all too aware that the very popular teacher whose place I had taken at Highfield was active in the Air Force and that he was receiving letters every week both from some of his old pupils and from his colleagues.

And then Neville intervened again in my life in the late autumn of 1941. Why not use my waiting time to teach at Keighley Grammar School, teaching, among others, candidates for scholarships and exhibitions at Cambridge and Oxford (the order he still put them in)? I did not hesitate, and at once found myself in the senior common room of the school where I had so recently been just along the corridor in the prefects' room, which I confess seemed more comfortable. My new colleagues included several who had not been there in 1938. One was Dick Hammond, an excellent historian, thoroughly unhappy to be teaching in a classroom which he could never control, anathema to Neville, but soon to leave to become official historian of the Ministry of Food. There he became sceptical about official histories, as I always was. By a coincidence a senior civil servant in the ministry was Martin Roseveare, father of Bob Roseveare. He was said to have invented the ration card and the points system.

By a further coincidence, at an Intelligence Corps Field Security course in Matlock, I met another person who had taught me French at school, Jim Siddle. Most of the people in the Intelligence Corps at that time were being directed into Field Security. Had Keighley Grammar School possessed an Officer Training Corps, as most public schools did, I would probably never have been at Matlock at all and the rest of my military life would have been quite different from what it was to be.

As it was, having reached my landmark twenty-first birthday on 7 May 1942 without a party I was called up, in routine fashion, and asked to report to the Royal Corps of Signals at Catterick Camp on 4 June 1942. I was a signalman before I was transferred into the Intelligence Corps. I travelled to Catterick from my grandmother's house in the village of East Morton near the edge of Ilkley Moor along with a farm boy from the village, Fred Clarkson, whom I had never met before. Having reported, one of the first tasks we had to carry out was to write a brief account of our lives before being called up and I was surprised to see that Fred, sitting next to me, was copying out what I was writing, it seemed to me word for word. The only difference between my account and his was that his handwriting was better than mine. He did not have time to finish his version of my life story, not being able to keep up with me, and he was quickly detailed to join a transport section, not to become a signalman dealing with radio and with Morse as I was to do.

The second of our tasks was to undergo a far from thorough medical examination, and I then had a different kind of surprise when one of the strongest-looking boys in my platoon – he came from Bradford – was told to get out of uniform, go home at once and stay there. I subsequently discovered that, because of his work in the wool trade, he was judged to be a carrier of anthrax.

My brief stay in Catterick was a happy one, and I learnt much about radio and Morse that was to prove useful to me later in life. I made several good friends, with whom I kept in touch, before moving at the end of the course from Catterick to Trowbridge in Wiltshire, where I started Y Service training as an interceptionist. This proved useful to me far sooner, as I have noted in my last chapter. When I moved from the Intelligence Corps to BP I was one of the only people in Hut Six who had any Y Service experience. My Morse was good, and I knew, too, as everyone working with me in the watch, that German radio operators were capable of making foolish mistakes.

From the start Welchman, founder of the hut, had appreciated how important it was to develop good relations with the Y Service, on his own initiative visiting the Army's radio-intercept station in the old fort outside Chatham, a town more often associated with the Navy than with the Army. He made friends with the officer-in-charge, Lieutenant Commander Ellingworth, who explained to him for the first time how German radio networks operated, what were the duties of the German operators, and what were the characteristics of short-wave transmissions. They agreed that they would telephone each other every day and keep a register of interceptions.

Soon afterwards, Welchman invited Ellingworth to BP to spend a night, when he saw the first decodes of messages intercepted the previous day. Together they identified what came to be called 'Welchman specials', particular messages selected by John Coleman in charge of BP's Intercept Control Room. As the volume of radio traffic increased enormously in 1940 and 1941 Chatham proved too exposed to attacks from the air, and most of Ellingworth's team of highly experienced and dedicated inter-ceptors moved to Beaumanor in Leicestershire, fifty miles to the north of BP, to which it was linked by teleprinter circuits.

There were 'huts' there, so designated, as there were in BP, all of the interception huts being provided with underground pneumatic tubes leading to a control hut. Some messages were carried to BP by despatch riders, a shorter journey than the journey from Chatham. It took me time to learn the details of this intricate system of communication when I moved to BP, but I quickly got to know of the work being carried out at the large RAF interception station at Chicksands, east of BP, where in August 1942 the male operators under the command of Wing Commander Shepherd were augmented by WAAF operators. WAAFs became a major element in BP's personnel, and later in 1942 an auxiliary WAAF station was opened in Shaftesbury, Dorset.

At this point, and indeed earlier, institutional memories become mingled with personal memories. My future wife, born in Devizes, was at a village school outside Trowbridge when I was learning Morse there in the Royal Horse Artillery Barracks (and on occasion guarding its town hall) and moved on to St Mary's Convent School, Shaftesbury, where there was a satellite station for Chicksands.

When I returned to the Intelligence Corps depot after Matlock I was told very quickly to report for another course in Bedford. I was not informed what its subject would be. It turned out to be cryptography. It might well have been Japanese. The idea of organizing such Japanese courses came not from Welchman but from Tiltman, who defied expert linguisticians who told him that Japanese linguists could not be trained in six months. The need to recruit more talented young graduates was pressing. My Bedford course was in no sense, however, an initiation into the kind of work I would be doing in BP, and I was the only person in my group to follow it up by going into Hut Six. The others included Alexander Lieven, who after the war was to head the BBC's Russian Service, and Alexander Hyatt King, director of the music section of the British Museum. Both of them remained close friends after the end of the war, but we never once talked about BP.

## Chapter 4

# The Huts – and Hut Six in Particular

The first and for decades the only written account of code-breaking work in Hut Six, then kept secret, was drafted shortly after the end of the war. It was in three volumes and was edited by Stuart Milner-Barry who also wrote a 25-page 'General Retrospect' at the beginning of Volume I. The whole work was dated 29 September 1945. Confusingly the three volumes were divided into four 'books'. These started with a description of the Enigma machine (we do not know who wrote that), and Book 1 continued with a chronological survey of Hut Six activities. Pages 29–79, by an anonymous author, cover what are called 'the early years'.

These were to be covered more fully in Welchman's book *The Hut Six Story*, a no longer secret account, which was published in 1982 by McGraw-Hill in the United States and by Allen Lane in Britain. The American edition lost Welchman his security clearance in the United States, nor was the book approved of by GCHQ in Cheltenham, which foolishly threatened him with prosecution. The authorities judged that he was giving too much away. Immediately after the end of the war, in that first secret account, Milner-Barry had paid Welchman fulsome tributes for his various achievements, and these he repeated and sharpened in a piece he wrote for Hinsley and Stripp in 1993. 'If Gordon Welchman had not been there', he claimed, 'I doubt if Ultra would have played the part that it undoubtedly did in shortening the war.'

My own BP perspectives were, as I have already explained, those of Hut Six (cryptography), but it was long after I left BP that I read Milner-Barry's account, which focuses on Welchman and deliberately picks out for mention only a few other Hut Six characters. Since Milner-Barry knew that a parallel account of Hut Three (intelligence) was being written, also in secret, he had rather less to say about relations between Hut Three and Hut Six than Welchman who created them both. Hut Eight, which like Hut Six was concerned with breaking Enigma (principally naval cyphers), was outside his range of reference. So too was Hut Four, which like Hut Three was concerned with intelligence, but which also broke various hand cyphers and some Italian naval traffic.

Milner-Barry's conclusion, which avoided comparisons, was honest and, to me, when I first read it – and now – in general convincing:

> Hut 6 was fortunate in its birth, and more fortunate in the job it had to do; most fortunate of all in that by a series of coincidences and lucky chances, mistakes galore by the enemy mixed with his superb efficiency, it was enabled to do its job to the end.

I said that Milner-Barry's conclusion avoided comparisons but he could not quite escape from a comparison, in his case concealed, with Germany. We now have enough knowledge of the German war machine to recognize, as he did, that not only did the men who operated it make many mistakes but that the machine itself had some weaknesses.

In accounting for how Hut Six did its work he attached importance to 'the personal aspect' of the organization:

A small body coming together in a time of desperate urgency is bound together by ties much closer and more intimate than can be found in a larger and more impersonal organisation. It was the common determination of all to strive to preserve something of this atmosphere, however vast and complex the organisation became.

Even in other huts where there was more complex organization along with more personal tensions than there were in Hut Six there was a sense of sharing in common tasks – as there was in BP as a whole, large parts of it dealing with the breaking of cyphers other than Enigma, including both the non-Morse-based Fish cyphers and a range of hand cyphers, among them Playfair types, which I thought I had left behind me when I exchanged my cryptography course in a converted Bedford house for Hut Six of BP.

It was Welchman who devised the whole Hut system at BP, beginning with Hut Six which Welchman himself was to head. Hut Six and Hut Three were together to be at the hub of the BP system. It was not clear then how many other huts there would have to be in the distant future. Yet Welchman did not introduce physical hut buildings to BP, for these go back to the time when the Bletchley Park estate was acquired by a syndicate at an auction held in July 1937, before Admiral Sinclair had decided to acquire BP for intelligence purposes. The leading figure in the syndicate, Captain Hubert Faulkner, an energetic local builder, had set about building huts before the change of ownership. He wished to get rid of the Mansion, along with some of the stables and cottages and to develop the property for residential use.

When ownership changed and Captain Ridley's so-called shooting party arrived in August 1938 to look at the property for

Sinclair, Faulkner had already demolished one wing in the stable-yard and had started converting stables into cottages and flats; and after having deciding to stay on the site after its transfer to GC&CS, he visited it once or twice a day. He went on to construct six single-storey wooden huts between the Munich crisis of 1938 and the rehearsal for the wartime move of GC&CS from London which began on 15 August 1939. The fact that Faulkner was a 'keen horseman' endeared him to Welchman, who at once realized – of far greater importance – that he knew how to handle bricklayers, builders and carpenters and make use of local skills. One of his carpenters, Bob Watson, then aged twenty, was to work at BP and its out-stations for nearly forty-five years.

The word 'hut', Welchman pointed out in *The Hut Six Story*, had many meanings. Faulkner's huts had the advantage for Welchman that they were entirely functional in character. They varied in width, and they were all capable of partitioning, with different sections being divided by plasterboard. This was also used on the inside walls. Design was simple. In most of the huts there was a poky central passageway with two large rooms at the end. There were no extras and no frills. The furniture consisted only of tables and stacking chairs. It did not matter to Faulkner, who had devised the internal layout, that in order to go to the toilet staff working in a hut would have to go into another building. This would not be the Mansion, where there were the most ornate toilets in BP, devised by Sir Herbert Leon. By the time I was to get to BP the Mansion was usually called less grandiloquently the Main Building.

Denniston was apparently little involved in the planning of the Huts, and it was Travis and his administrator, Commander A. R. Bradshaw, who took responsibility for them. There were to be problems for the people who were to work in them. In the section on which Welchman called 'backdrop' in *The Hut Six Story* no reference was made to the heating of the huts. In winter they were too cold, in summer too hot, and from the start the blacked-out windows had to be taped and there was too little light. The light bulbs had no shades. The noise that builders made as more and more huts were built, creating what was thought of as a 'huddle of huts', could be deeply disturbing to those working inside them. The smells from the fires were totally obnoxious and the fumes possibly dangerous.

Welchman did not concern himself much about the numbering of the Huts, 'once', as he put it 'huts were being built all over the place'. Nor, he added, 'should the reader' of *The Hut Six Story* bother about the purposes for which Huts 1, 2, 3, 4, etc. were built or what went on in them. It would be too confusing. The numbers attached to the actual wooden structures kept being changed so that a section could continue to be known by the same hut number when it moved to new quarters. Welchman did mention Hut Eight four times, however, if briefly. It dealt with the breaking of Naval Enigma which had a distinctive place in cryptography and in war strategy, and when in February 1943 Huts Six and Three moved into a new brick block, Block D, Huts Eight and Four moved with them.

In the long run, Welchman recognized that there might have to be more permanent buildings than huts, and the long run proved to be less long than he thought, for Elmers School, a former country house converted into a private school and taken over by GC&CS in 1939, was bombed on 21 November 1940, the one occasion during the war when any bombs fell on Bletchley. Faulkner's mind had already moved in a similar direction to Welchman's, but neither of them had any idea of what the timing of any strategic moves would be.

Faulkner had never pulled down the Mansion or built a new house for himself to replace it on the lawn by the lake. He appreciated that the organization which had now acquired BP, the full purposes of which he could not have understood, would find it necessary to retain, though drastically to change, the existing Mansion, ugly and pretentious though it seemed to be to him and many of the Park's new inhabitants. Some cottages, he believed, might be converted to office use, and so, indeed, might some of the stables.

Dilly Knox moved at once into a cottage, which thereafter was usually called 'The Cottage', and Turing into a stableboy's loft above a stable. In these initial moves there was no room for Welchman in 'The Cottage' and he had been placed in Elmers School. In this initial period in BP Knox told him nothing about the Polish prelude to the breaking of Enigma. Nor did he tell him of how he himself had broken messages encyphered on a simpler Enigma machine used by Franco and Mussolini during the Spanish Civil War.

Welchman had a different conception from Knox about what would be needed at BP in the future. During the German attack on Poland he had been impressed by German radio communications skills. (In *The Hut Six Story* he was to choose as his first illustration a photograph, frequently to be reproduced by other writers, among them Lewin, of Panzer General Guderian's command vehicle complete with two Enigma machines and their young operators.) This suggested to him that, as war became more mobile, the use of the Enigma would increase. Landline communication would give way increasingly to radio communication. He did not go on, however, to consider the effects of radio silence on the work of both Huts Six and Three. For a variety of reasons the number of Enigma messages intercepted in Britain would fluctuate rather than follow a completely consistent pattern and this would affect decryption rates. Continuity in breaking keys was very desirable both for Hut Three and Hut Six.

Knox had demonstrated that he had more than cryptographic skills when he established close liaison with Bruno, the code-name for the group of Polish radio intelligence officers working in exile in France. For a time Henri Braquenié, a French cryptographer, worked with him in The Cottage. Braquenié was employed by Gustave Bertrand, the French intelligence officer who supervised the exiled Poles in France. In the Château de Vignolles, thirty-five miles north-east of Paris, they worked assiduously on Enigma. Captain Kenneth Macfarlan, an experienced British signals intelligence officer, was attached to them.

In the place where Welchman had been put, the requisitioned Elmers School, he worked on parallel lines to Knox, who was trying to break Enigma by using a system of perforated sheets, devised by the Poles, who had to do the perforating themselves by hand, using a razor blade. By contrast Knox could order large numbers of perforated sheets to be made inside BP using a special machine, and a full set of these was sent out to Bruno in the Château de Vignolles. They were essential to their operations. Alan Turing was the emissary, and he was already envisaging a quite different way of breaking Enigma.

Years later Welchman was to declare that he had not been upset about Knox's attempts to exclude him from trying to break Enigma, and he welcomed the fact that Knox transferred John Jeffreys, a research fellow in mathematics of Downing College, Cambridge, who was a friend of Turing, to work with him in Elmers. Nevertheless, he had been and remained unhappy about Knox's approach to what he called 'research'. He did not think that Knox was in any sense an 'organization man' or that he had much interest in what Welchman, with an industrial model in mind, called 'production'. For Knox breaking a cypher was a triumph of individual genius: for Welchman, who did not disparage genius, it was less a matter of breaking a message in cypher, more of breaking whatever range of cyphers the enemy employed. For Welchman a supply of intelligence to the limited number of customers who needed it was the end product at BP. Over the years his systematic approach was shared by others, including some of the people in Hut Three. They thought, as he did, in terms of a production 'flow of urgent operational intelligence'.

Before BP had broken a single Enigma message, Welchman, not yet himself a cryptographer, convinced Edward Travis, who before the war had been head of cypher security at GC&CS and was now second-in-command to Alastair Denniston, that breaking Enigma messages on a large scale would require the production of machines to cope with machines. The Poles had invented what they called bombas; the machines which he and Turing were envisaging would be called 'bombes'. Their machines were different in character from bombas, and if BP were to introduce practical bombes that would work a great deal of extra expenditure would be required. The scale of operations at BP would need to be transformed. This was still the period called by an American 'the phoney war', but Welchman knew that it would not be phoney for long. It was not. On 9 April Hitler invaded Denmark and Norway.

It was a sign of Travis's political skill, as important a factor in his personal success as his indomitable energy, that he persuaded Whitehall in the curious circumstances of 1939 to fund BP's bombe-making. On 18 November, therefore, he sent a note to Denniston proposing that Knox's research section should be split off from a new production section. Denniston, who appreciated

Welchman's qualities, agreed to the split. He was preoccupied with other problems following the move to BP, but since he knew Knox far better than Welchman he did not immediately agree to any suggestion that Welchman would head the second section. Nor did Travis press for this. Nevertheless, fully supported by Travis, what was now called Hut Six, the headquarters of the production section, no longer described as such, was opened in January 1940. Welchman quickly took it over, making its Machine Room the main driving force behind the development of analytical machines to speed up the decryption process.

Knox's methods of breaking Enigma by the use of perforated sheets became impossible after May 1940, for, soon after their invasion of Holland, Belgium and France, the Germans made a simple change in the Enigma encrypting procedure. Double encypherment of the wheel setting of Enigma largely ceased and a new approach to breaking Enigma became essential. At the same time it became impossible to maintain close liaison with the Polish cryptographers who, having moved to France after the collapse of Poland, now, after the collapse of France in June 1940, were being forced to move again to a château in the town of Uzès not far from the Mediterranean in unoccupied Provence.

The brilliant Polish cryptographer Henryk Zygalski, who had devised the perforated sheet system, was kept completely in the dark about what was happening in Welchman's Hut Six, even though in 1943 he was to leave France and work in England attached to the Polish Army. It was not until he read Winterbotham's *The Ultra Secret* in 1974 that he had any conception of the scale of BP's wartime operations or of its record of success. After the war he moved permanently to Britain not as a soldier but as an 'academic'. His last post was as a lecturer in mathematics at the University of Surrey, where his colleagues learned no more of his penetration of the Enigma machine before the war than he knew of wartime BP.

There would have been much for Zygalski to learn, for before the collapse of France BP, in dramatic but difficult times, gradually took shape as an integrated whole. Hut Eight, concerned with naval code-breaking, worked in parallel with Hut Six. Hut Eight was headed at first by Turing, but there were few breaks into Naval Enigma (Dolphin) in 1940. Hut Six had been more successful. Thanks to Welchman's inspired discovery, described in *The Hut Six Story*, of what he called the diagonal board, and to his pupil John Herivel's brilliant idea of the Herivel Tip, which dramatically narrowed down the number of likely ring settings that the German operators might employ, Hut Six was regularly breaking by hand the main German Enigma key called Red, with very few gaps day by day from May 1940. This was not just the basic Luftwaffe key but the prime source of intelligence concerning Germany's war effort. Another Welchman pupil, David Rees, called the Herivel Tip 'seminal'. The subsequent breaking of a large number of keys by machine depended on earlier hand breaking of a smaller core of keys. They had thrown up 'cribs' that could be fed to bombes.

The arrival at BP on 18 March 1940 of Turing's first experimental bombe, optimistically called Victory, was a landmark date not only in the history of BP but in the history of cryptography, though there was no thought then that it would be followed by an even greater landmark day for Britain and the world, 18 January 1944, described below, when the first Colossus arrived in BP. Colossus would be a computer, a word not in use in its present sense in 1940. The bombe was a device that exploited the electrical circuitry of an Enigma machine by using an electrical method to reveal when an encrypted message had been broken with the help of a crib. Bombes were constructed not at BP or by any government establishment but by BTM, the British Tabulating Machine Company, located in Letchworth. Associated with the American company IBM, BTM drew on a wide range of sub-contractors, kept completely in the dark, of course, about what they were doing.

Welchman, whose so-called 'diagonal board was a vital feature in the production of subsequent bombes, found it easier than Turing to work closely with the leading BTM engineer, Harold Keene, known as 'Doc Keene', who was largely responsible for producing and designing later bombes to make them more practicable than Victory. Yet it was people in BP who encouraged and made possible the production of more and more bombes, notably Harold Fletcher, who dealt with the management aspects of the bombe programmes, and Sergeant, later Squadron Leader, Jones (not the Eric Jones who was to become head of a troubled Hut Three in July 1942 and later, after the war, head of GCHQ) who handled any technical problems that Hut Six might throw at him.

How best securely to move the first BTM bombe from Letchworth to BP was not easy to decide upon, and even after Victory arrived safely at BP there were different kinds of difficulties ahead, the first physical. The doorway of the northern end of Hut One, a hut first designed to accommodate BP's wireless station, had to be widened to allow access. This difficulty, along with security considerations, encouraged the placing of most further bombes outside BP in out-stations, which were known by their initials.

The hut was a crowded place, shared between what was called at first Squadron Leader Jones's section and the sick bay. Jones had only two people working with him, one representing the Navy and one the Army (he himself represented the Air Force) and their room measured 15 feet by 12 feet. It was known by many names, including the I/c Ops, the Powder Room, and even The Office. The basic name 'section' was quickly to be used in many parts of BP. Indeed, sections were as integral a part of BP organization as Huts.

Victory, the first bombe to arrive, had serious technical limitations, although it was out of action for only 42 hours in its first 14 months at BP; and on 8 August 1940 a new type of Turing bombe, Agnes (or sometimes Agnus, from *Agnus Dei*), affectionately nicknamed Aggie, was installed. It was fitted with Welchman's diagonal board and was designed by Doc Keene. Through many trials and tribulations it remained operational to the last. All the later bombes were given names, and after Wrens were appointed to look after them in March 1941, it was they who chose the names. Victorious was no advance on Victory: Warspite sounded contemporary, as did all the names of fighter aircraft. By the end of the war there were to be 1,676 Wrens in six different out-stations around the country. Many of them have told their own stories. One of the first of them, Diana Paine, had joined the WRNS dreaming of the sea and marrying a sailor.

Welchman insisted that the bombes did not break the Enigma keys, the number of which increased greatly in 1942 and 1943. The 'credit' had to go not to the machines but to the Wrens who had to tend them and to the code-breakers who had to feed them. Bombes, he maintained, were ancillary instruments, useless without 'cribs' – sections of text that the code-breakers anticipated would be included in the signals. Milner-Barry in Hut Six was clever in finding them. In Hut Eight, where a Crib Room was set up in 1941, headed by Shaun Wylie, the people handling them were called cribsters.

The cribs that cribsters selected were of various kinds, some easy to pick out, some difficult. Hunches mattered, although the

Germans assisted the cribsters by using stereotyped beginnings and ends of messages and by sending some messages, such as weather reports, at the same time each day. Some messages included slogans or quotations, including 'Heil Hitler', and nonsense, often described as such by the operator. Some were translations or repeats of other messages. One Enigma operator helpfully reported day after day that he had nothing to report – '*Nicht zu melden.*'

Historians could make excellent cribsters since they were usually well-read, drawn to lateral thinking, and taught to get inside the mind of people totally different from themselves. Senders were good prey. Many Y Service interceptors would have made good cribsters too. They were capable of imagining what their German opposite numbers were like by tracking their habits and styles which did not change when there were changes in the frequencies they were using and even the keys. Many what might be thought of as 'hunches' were genuine insights. Concentration and insight were almost as valuable BP qualities as mathematics, and fortunately many mathematicians, such as Herivel, possessed them.

There was, of course, a technical side to cribbing also. Turning cribs into 'menus' with which the bombes were fed would have been almost impossible had there not been three features of the Enigma machine that even totally non-machine-minded crypto-graphers knew about. First, the machine would never show up the same letter in an encrypted message as was there in the original text. A would never appear as A; any other letter was possible. Second, the letter coding was reciprocal: if A appeared as B, B would appear as A. Third, Enigma did not encrypt numbers: the numbers always had to be spelt out in letters.

Had the Germans employed machines that lacked these char-acteristics their messages would have been far trickier to decypher.

Likewise – and this had nothing to do with the make-up of a machine – it would have been difficult for decypherers to find enough letters to make up a menu from a crib had not the Germans liked to incorporate the names, ranks and addresses of the senders and receivers in their texts. They also liked going over old ground in standard format when they dealt with supply, administration and planned schedules.

On the decrypting side Hut Six needed as many messages as possible to try to break a key and more and more bombes to try to break any key. In March 1941 there were only four bombes in use; Travis, who called bombes 'spiders', wanted to have forty to fifty. By the end of 1941 there were sixteen; by the end of 1942 forty-nine; and at the end of 1943 there were ninety-nine. They were supplemented by American bombes, although none of these crossed the Atlantic. It was not until 26 May 1943, however, that the first of two American new prototype bombes, Adam and Eve, came into use. Faster than their British counterparts, they were manufactured by National Cash Register (NCR) in Dayton, Ohio.

Meanwhile BTM speeded up its own production processes. The first bombes took five weeks to construct; later bombes, built in batches of six, left the assembly line at the rate of one a week.

Wrens were employed to tend the bombes for the first time in March 1941, eight of them as an experiment, and the section moved from Hut One to Hut Eleven. Out-station Adstock also came into operation. By the end of 1942 there were 571 Wrens. Out-station Stanmore was opened in November 1942. It consisted of ten bays each as large as a new Hut 11a, opened next to Hut Eleven in the previous February.

All the history of bombes was new to me when I arrived in BP in the early summer of 1943. I very soon took it for granted. For Welchman, summing it up years later, there were three periods in the history of the use of bombes. The first began in September 1940, when the prototype bombe Victory arrived improved from Letchworth to be installed not in BP itself but in the village of Wavendon. This period lasted until December 1941 and the second period, equally roughly dated, covered the whole of the year 1942, when there was a jump in the number of keys that the Germans were using and when the number of people working at BP and its out-stations increased even more rapidly. The period ended in mid-February 1943 when a huge new Block D, 40,000 square feet of space, then the biggest building in BP, was opened. The third period, which to me was real history in most of which I participated, lasted from then until the end of the war. There was no real break in it when Welchman left Hut Six to become ADMech. The name Hut Six survived his move as it did the opening of the new block.

People like me who started breaking Enigma in the improved conditions offered in the new centrally heated, well-lit block constituted a new BP cohort, being treated quite differently from previous intakes in the old single-storey wooden Hut Six. Nevertheless, those intakes, now experienced BPites, were at our side and for our part we maintained the same team spirit that had been so conspicuous earlier in the old. The work that we were all doing was essentially the same as that done before 1943. Routines had long been established. As Derek Taunt observed, the Hut operated like a factory which never switched off its own assembly line.

We were dependent on radio interception, as Hut Six had always been: it was the basis of all that we could do. Once the messages had been intercepted in different places in what were often disturbing, sometimes intimidating local conditions, they arrived in Hut Six to be registered, the dullest of all BP routines, and made their way through all the intervening rooms in Hut Six to Hut Three. Newcomers to Hut Six, whatever they were doing, knew at once that there was a story behind it. They were not encouraged, however, to learn much about it, to discover how the routines in the Hut were related to each other or, indeed, what other people were doing in other 'rooms' inside the Hut. Only members of the Watch were allowed to know, or rather they were required to know what everyone inside the Hut was doing.

For me there seemed to be no continuity between what I learned on my cryptographic course in Bedford, which had been concerned, as I said in my last chapter, only with hand and not with machine cyphers, and what I was now doing in the Hut Six Watch. I was in a mood of mingled excitement and trepidation, therefore, when I got down to work. The first thing that struck me and rather alarmed me on my first day in Hut Six was the large number of telephones on the table in front of me in the room where I was to work. I was totally unused to different telephones ringing while I was answering a telephone call on another. Nor had I ever seen so many machines, or women working them, as I did in the adjacent Machine Room, or MR as we all called it, since as a boy in Keighley I had been inside textile mills full of women.

In the Machine Room I encountered far better educated women, most of whom seemed around the same age as myself. They were separated from me by a hatch and beyond it a door. Nobody told me much about what they were doing on the other side of the hatch or what their shift leader would say to me when she opened it. I guessed that the machines that the women were working were German Enigmas and that the hatch would be opened if a code was broken. I was wrong on the first count but right on the second. The machines looked like Enigmas but were made in Britain, being modified versions of our own Typex machines. The Machine Room did tell us when a key had been broken.

On our side of the hatch our main but by no means our sole task was to find testable cribs and to prepare menus from them. The first three BPite words I learned in the Watch were 'Watch' itself, 'crib' and 'menu'. The first word was, I knew, connected with the Navy, and the second stirred schoolboy memories of cribs that we used in translating Latin or that some of us carried secretly into examinations. The third word, however, was more than a word though I had for years studied menus hopefully in English restaurants and more agreeably in French restaurants.

The term Watch I quickly took for granted, and I came to know that the BP Wrens were forced to use it when they were outside BP as well as in it. As for cribs I did not appreciate until I started working on Enigma cribs how varied their origins could be or how I would enjoy identifying them. For menus, I was never to be totally impressed by menus in the BP cafeteria which had been opened in 1942, though they were better than those in British Restaurants. But I enjoyed writing cryptographic menus and was delighted if I wrote a correct one that made a bombe stop and revealed the Enigma machine settings not only for the whole message but for all the messages on that key.

The women on the other side of the hatch knew as much about menus for bombes as we did, and it was the task of the head of shift sitting beside the hatch in the Machine Room to keep a list of which menu was being fed into which bombe and where. It was our task, not theirs, to find cribs. Our work patterns, however, were the same. On each side of the hatch we operated on a three-shift system with flexible rotas: there was no reason why the same shift members on each side would work together regularly. By the time I arrived we on the Watch had shift leaders working on a rota basis – Howard Smith was one – but, unlike ourselves, the Machine Room had a regular section head, Mary Wilson, highly capable and deeply committed to cooperation with the Watch. She was more than a shift leader.

The shift leader in the Machine Room communicated directly with BP's out-stations where the bombes were kept, such as Wavendon, Adstock, Gayhurst and Stanmore. The menus were wired up there, and the bombes rattled noisily and at great speed through a myriad of possible wheel orders. Then, if a menu was correct, a bombe would 'stop' (another BP term) at a position where all the links on the menu had been confirmed. The out-station would then telephone the shift leader in the Machine Room and a member of the shift there would immediately set up one of the MR's Enigma-like machines first to confirm that the stop fitted the menu and, second, to key in a few more letters to see whether the decrypted German message made sense.

The Watch would then be informed through the hatch that the key in which the message had been sent had been broken. The main key, regularly broken, was Red, and the cry 'Red's up', the first cry of exclamation that I heard in the Watch, excited us as much as it comforted the members of Hut Three. Having heard it, the MR's shift leader would telephone the out-stations to instruct them to strip all of their bombes that were handling Red menus so that they could be freed to deal with menus in other keys.

The names of the keys were chosen in the Watch, and we liked choosing them. When colours ran out – and coloured pencils had run out long before I arrived – the names chosen might be insects, birds or animals. Gadfly, Hornet, Wasp, Locust and Cockroach had been among the first insect names chosen early in 1942.

If and when the keys were broken, messages were then passed on to Hut Six's Decoding Room (DR) and after that to Hut Three for action. Some of the messages tested would prove to be 'duds', a BP technical term in Hut Six: for whatever reason, it had not been able to decypher them. The Decoding Room was one of the oldest sections in Hut Six. It started life with one machine, modified from a British Typex cypher machine, and a staff of two. By September 1941, however, there were about a dozen machines. The section moved several times before settling permanently in Block D in February 1943, and I was told by one or two of its most long-standing members that when they started work in DR there had been a three-minute walk from there to get to Hut Three.

After Hut Six and Hut Three moved side by side decoded traffic was pushed in trays down a covered hatchway between the two huts, known as the DR Tunnel. In Block D, however, there was a conveyor belt, which, rumour went, was based on a similar belt in the John Lewis store in London. In September 1942 a Decoding Room school was created where newcomers to the room learned about traffic flow and machine maintenance.

The following year, in August 1943, one month after I arrived in Hut Six, the two jobs of Head of the Decoding Room and Hut Six Duty Officer were combined, but they were to be separated again in April 1944, well before D-Day, owing to the large expansion of the section as a whole. The two persons shared an office, however, and worked in close association, deputizing for each other when necessary. Meanwhile, rotating heads of shift kept up-to-date what was called the Fracture Book, which recorded details of broken keys. They were responsible too for time-stamping the arrival of each message. I spent more time in the Decoding Room than in the Machine Room, chatting to girls who had frequently been highly educated.

Harold Fletcher, high above, was in charge of both sections and of the Registration Room, consisting entirely of women, and both Welchman and Milner-Barry had the highest opinion of his way with dealing with them. Without having had any formal instruction and without meeting Fletcher I quickly learned for myself what the relationship between the two women's sections was and what were the relations between each of them and the Watch that linked them. I noted that there was a relatively high rate of mobility from the Registration Room to other rooms, for the work in the Registration Room was held to be more boring. Yet some members were more cheerful than others. A high proportion were resigned to their lot and showed no inclination to move. There was no great desire to become a shift leader. The Machine Room was the elite room, the Decoding Room a place for the occupationally ambitious. Women working in there judged the Watch by its individual members. Some members of the Watch did not understand women. Some fostered personal relationships with women that lasted. A few flirted.

I preferred flirting to asserting superiority, but I took seriously the reactions of individual women to their work. I felt that my judgements were often sounder than Milner-Barry's. When Welchman left Hut Six and Milner-Barry became its head in September 1943, Major John Manisty, whom I liked, became head of the Watch. He had a partitioned office of his own and a rather shy but able personal assistant, Wendy Hinde, who was an historian who after the war eventually became editor of *International Affairs*.

Manisty had come to the conclusion with no prompting, as I did later, that it would be useful if all newcomers to the Watch, male or female, or indeed to the women's sections, attended a fortnightly school to 'learn the ropes' and to get some sense of how the different sections of Hut Six – and these were to change more than once – were related to each other. The school I attended was run by Ione Jay, one year older than myself, whom I have introduced in a previous chapter. She had joined the

Registration Room in April 1941 and proved to be such a good teacher that Manisty wanted her to stay in the Watch to work there.

She did not choose to do so, but under his guidance she moved to a section of Hut Six next door to the Watch which was called the Qwatch, a pun on the German name for rubbish, *Quatsch*, and worked in a team of three with Derek Taunt and Arthur Read, recruited straight from Marlborough. I saw quite a lot of them, loving their propensity for pun-making while they were very seriously devising contingency plans to deal with possible new complications in German handling of Enigma. They studied, for example, emergency keys, *Notschlüsseln*, that the Germans might construct from long words.

Years later, in 2005, Ione wrote and published an account of her life, which she called *Things I Remember*. Her life had many twists and turns and took her to many places in the world, but BP, where she married a fellow member of Hut Six, Bob Roseveare, who joined the Watch in January 1942, played a pivotal part in it. Through a series of coincidences and contacts I got in touch with her in 2010 for only the second time since we both left BP in 1945, and she sent me a copy of her well-titled book, signed with love. Ione's book looked at Hut Six, as I do, largely from below, yet she had kept in touch with far more people in Hut Six than I did, among them Bill Bundy, the head of the American group that arrived in Hut Six a few weeks after me.

Like Ione, during the last stages of the war I got to know well the group of American newcomers who entered BP on 6 August 1943. Welchman himself gave a talk to the group in his office in Block D, describing Hut Six's work. He remembered the precise time of day he addressed them 'since they had travelled from London to Bletchley on the train leaving Euston at 3.06 p.m.', which was the same train that Harold Fletcher had caught exactly two years before. 'I felt somewhat ill at ease,' Welchman recalled,

> as I tried to tell them the Hut Six story. But their attitude was simply that they wanted to be told what to do so that they could be helpful as soon as possible. There were no fanfares. No arguments. No difficulties. They simply melted into Hut Six and were liked and welcomed by everyone. Very soon each of them had found a niche and was contributing.

I shall describe the Americans more fully in my next chapter. I should note at this point, however, that one of them, Al (Fred) Friendly, was a born story-teller who was to become managing editor of the *Washington Post*. He became a good friend!

I myself had found my own niche before the Americans arrived and Welchman left Hut Six. Each of us in the Watch was requested to adopt one key of our own in the same way as across the Atlantic Americans adopt one mile of a highway. Mine was Puma, a Luftwaffe key that offered me a watching brief on Yugoslavia, then an immensely interesting country to observe. The Chiefs of Staff in London and the Joint Intelligence Committee were sent paraphrases of decrypted German messages relating to what was happening there under strict conditions of security, but not until the autumn of 1943 did these go to SOE or the Foreign Office.

By then I felt almost directly involved myself in the fierce Partisan struggles that were splitting our own intelligence agents sent out to the Balkans. The volume of BP decrypts was enormous in 1943, among the most important of them Abwehr messages, broken outside Hut Six. On 11 July, Churchill, who was receiving conflicting intelligence from a variety of sources, had instructed that a 2,000- to 3,000-word digest of sigint information about Yugoslavia should be sent to him.

In the decisive autumn of that year all my own sympathies were with Tito, although there were powerful voices in London warning the Allies not to deal with him. I have remained deeply interested in Yugoslavia ever since. I remained interested too, although for a much shorter time, in the German air force commanders who provided me with my secret information. Their names were so well known to me that I hoped I would meet some of them face-to-face after the end of the war. I never did.

Finding a wartime niche did not in any way preclude my being involved in the wide range of tasks carried out in common by Watch shifts. These were allotted by the shift leader on a rota basis with a division of labour on each shift. We sat on hard chairs at separate but not individual tables. One person provided the link with the Machine Room, as I had done on my first day in BP. Another kept a log book of happenings on the shift. A third sat at the point on the conveyor belt where broken messages came in, scanned them speedily and passed them on to Hut Three. At choice moments finding cribs could be fun. If there was infor- mation to pass over to the next shift – or problems – we would write it down. There was little time to talk when shifts changed.

Perhaps more than any other member of the Watch, because of my interest in current politics and in contemporary history, I appreciated most the liaison between the Watch in Hut Six and Hut Three. There were stirring events between the day I arrived and D-Day the following year. In July 1943 British and American troops invaded Sicily, where, again putting public and private history together, I was to spend my honeymoon twelve years later. In September Russian forces swept forward and advanced to the River Don, crossing it in places. In October HMS *Charybdis* and

HMS *Limbourne* were lost fighting blockade runners off the Channel Islands, the only occupied British territory, the wartime history of which I was to record in a book to celebrate the jubilee of their liberation. In November the Teheran Conference began: it was to figure prominently in the book I was already planning in 1943, *Patterns of Peacemaking*. In December the Allies were closing in on Monte Cassino.

Observing all this from the Hut Six Watch, the war was always alive. I know that the word Watch meant different things in Hut Six and Hut Three. In Hut Six there was one Watch: in Hut Three there were no fewer than five watches, each consisting of a No. 1, a No. 2 and five or six other members. Hut Three watches worked on a regular ten-day cycle. There were also 'specialist' and 'permanent backroom watches', one dealing with Balkan intelligence and one with Russian intelligence, one with the German Y service and one with secret weapons. One watch – and at the end of the war two – consisted entirely of women. They all had access to sources of information other than their main source, intercepted messages. 'The general principle of all watches', de Grey emphasized, 'was that nothing should be neglected if there were a faint possibility that it could prove of importance to someone at a Ministry or Command.'

The specialist and backroom watches worked more regular but longer hours than the operational watches, and while the work of the former was slower it was more thorough than that of the latter. For a time during the winter of 1942/3, when there had been a flow of new recruits to Hut Three, a special 'Training Watch' was in existence. Later in 1943 the flow became a flood, as we have seen, sweeping me into BP with it. Changing the terminology, both in Hut Six and in Hut Three a new cohort entered BP after I arrived. I cannot, however, recall any wartime comparisons between the new cohort in Hut Six and the new cohort in Hut Three. We were too busy in our own Huts to probe what was common to us both.

The Hut Three Watch consisted of about a dozen people sitting round a semi-circular table, with the head of the Watch sitting inside the semi-circle facing his colleagues. All of them knew German. When messages arrived from Hut Six a member of the Hut Three Watch took each one, separated the five-letter groups into German words by pencil strokes and wrote down an English version of the text on a separate piece of paper. The head of the Watch meticulously checked the papers that they had given him and then, in turn, passed them on to the air and military advisors, working in pairs, who sat at an adjacent rectangular table.

The advisors had no counterparts in the Hut Six Watch. It was their two-fold task, a highly responsible one, to judge, first, what new intelligence each message provided and what was its significance, and, second, to draw up a version to pass on by signals to commanders in the field and by teleprinters to relevant ministries in London. Signals to commanders in the field were despatched over a special network, to SLUs, Special Liaison Units, consisting mainly of RAF personnel, and SCUs, Special Communications Units, manned mainly by the Army. The advisors, who saw every message that arrived in the Hut Three Watch, could pass on paraphrases and, if they so desired, add glosses preceded by the word 'Comment'. If they had not been able to do this their RAF and military recipients would have been swamped with information.

The system, which had its origins in April 1941, made sense, but I did not know, in the summer of 1943, when I was somewhat envious at times of work and life in Hut Three, how troubled and tense the history of Hut Three had been until Squadron Leader Eric Jones joined it in March 1942. I saw little of Jones myself, and

Built in several varieties the Enigma machine was first marketed in the 1920s. Adapted and developed as a military machine it went through a variety of phases. An Abwehr machine, borrowed from GCHQ, was stolen on an open day at BP in 2000. It was returned to Jeremy Paxman on 1 April 2002.

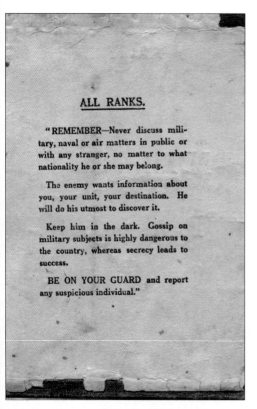

Good guidance to all ranks as printed in my own Army Paybook.

## ALL RANKS.

"REMEMBER—Never discuss military, naval or air matters in public or with any stranger, no matter to what nationality he or she may belong.

The enemy wants information about you, your unit, your destination. He will do his utmost to discover it.

Keep him in the dark. Gossip on military subjects is highly dangerous to the country, whereas secrecy leads to success.

BE ON YOUR GUARD and report any suspicious individual."

*Below left:* I was declared fit for military service in 1941 but my eyesight prevented me joining the Navy as I would have preferred.

*Below:* This Intelligence Corps Christmas menu from 1942 offers real food. I did not then know what a BP menu designed to feed a bombe would offer.

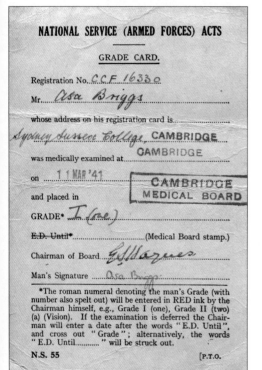

### NATIONAL SERVICE (ARMED FORCES) ACTS

#### GRADE CARD.

Registration No. *CCF 16330*

Mr. *Asa Briggs*

whose address on his registration card is..................

*Sydney Sussex College,* CAMBRIDGE

was medically examined at...... CAMBRIDGE

on ...... 1 1 MAR '41

and placed in

[CAMBRIDGE MEDICAL BOARD]

GRADE* *I (one)*

E.D. Until*..................(Medical Board stamp.)

Chairman of Board.....................

Man's Signature ...... *Asa Briggs*

*The roman numeral denoting the man's Grade (with number also spelt out) will be entered in RED ink by the Chairman himself, e.g., Grade I (one), Grade II (two) (a) (Vision). If the examination is deferred the Chairman will enter a date after the words "E.D. Until", and cross out "Grade"; alternatively, the words "E.D. Until........" will be struck out.

N.S. 55 [P.T.O.

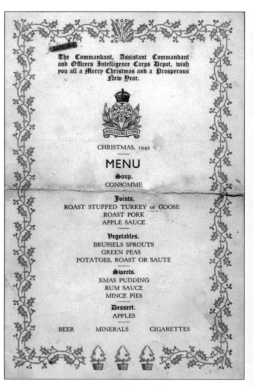

The Commandant, Assistant Commandant and Officers Intelligence Corps Depot, wish you all a Merry Christmas and a Prosperous New Year.

CHRISTMAS, 1942

## MENU

**Soup.**
CONSOMME

**Joints.**
ROAST STUFFED TURKEY or GOOSE
ROAST PORK
APPLE SAUCE

**Vegetables.**
BRUSSELS SPROUTS
GREEN PEAS
POTATOES, ROAST OR SAUTE

**Sweets.**
XMAS PUDDING
RUM SAUCE
MINCE PIES

**Dessert.**
APPLES

BEER    MINERALS    CIGARETTES

**B.P. RECREATIONAL CLUB**

Name **H͏ʳ BRIGGS**

**N⍛ 2350**

1. This Card must be carried and produced upon the request of a Club Official.

2. All resignations must be notified to the Secretary, accompanied by this Card.

---

**FORTHCOMING PRODUCTIONS
in this Theatre**

The Wolverton Club will present

**DANGEROUS CORNER**
by J. B. Priestley

on Saturday, 13th November.

The Drama Group will present their

**CHRISTMAS REVUE**

Probable Dates :

· Wednesday to Saturday,
Dec. 30th - Jan. 1st 1944,
AND
Monday to Wednesday,
Jan. 3rd - Jan. 5th 1944.

Warren, Printer, Bletchley.

---

*Above:* My ticket to all the leisure delights of BP. I paid for it in instalments, one shilling (5p) a month.

*Above right:* Drama in BP, along with a Christmas revue, 1943–4. Priestley was immensely popular.

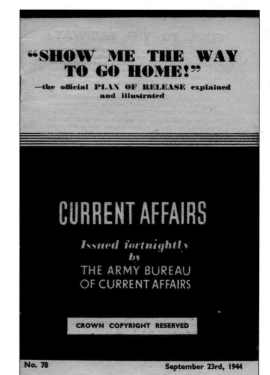

**"SHOW ME THE WAY TO GO HOME!"**
—the official PLAN OF RELEASE explained and illustrated

**CURRENT AFFAIRS**

*Issued fortnightly
by*
THE ARMY BUREAU
OF CURRENT AFFAIRS

**CROWN COPYRIGHT RESERVED**

No. 78                    September 23rd, 1944

*Right:* An ABCA pamphlet that we used at the Formation College. I kept a collection of these bulletins.

The entrance to the Mansion today. The first Station X was on the left.

Christine Large (*left*) and Mavis Batey at a BP function in 2004.

John Herivel (*standing at left*) and Mavis Batey (*seated*) with an Enigma machine during a Sue McGregor radio programme in London in 2008. I am on the right.

The Duke of Kent became patron of the Trust in 2002. He showed great interest in its work and enjoyed meeting old and new BPites.

*Above & left:* Views of the reconstructed bombe. The front view shows some of the drums and the interior views some of the wiring and other components and the contact brushes on the back of one of the drums.

*Above & right:* Interior and exterior views of the reconstructed Colossus I. In retrospect the original despatched Britain into a new digital age.

The service of wartime veterans was at last recognized in 2006 when people working in BP and its out-stations had badges designed for them.

Post-communist Poland has celebrated the breaking of Enigma by the issue of stamps and coins. The 1.95 zloty stamp shows three of the pioneer cryptographers, from top, Jerzy Różycki, Marian Rejewski and Henryk Zygalski.

while at BP I did not know of the magnitude of Jones's personal contribution to the achievement of order. Calvocoressi does not mention him once in *Top Secret Ultra*, but Ralph Bennett, one of the duty officers whom Jones appointed, paid an unqualified tribute to his 'firm but understanding rule . . . We could concentrate on our work undisturbed by internal conflict.'

It was long after I left BP that I began to piece together the story of pre-Jones Hut Three, of which I myself might well have been a member had it not been for Welchman. At first there were only four members of the Hut – a Navy commander, Malcolm Saunders; an RAF squadron leader, Robert Humphreys, senior liaison officer with the Air Force; Captain Curtis, senior liaison officer with the War Office, who knew no German; and Cambridge don, F. L. Lucas, the only one of them at all known in the outside world. Literary critic, poet and author as far back as 1929 of an acclaimed book *Time and Memory*, Lucas had been a member of the Intelligence Corps in the First World War.

The four men were not at all sure of what they were expected to do in the Second World War. They knew, however, before anyone except Dilly Knox broke an Enigma message, that they should draw the full meaning out of batches of decrypted messages sent to them in cardboard boxes from Hut Six, translate them into plain English and transmit what messages they thought relevant on to London – in their first days by open-line telephone with no scrambler devices. They knew too that when the messages arrived in London they might not be taken seriously. Their recipients might prefer to make their own judgements, relying on agents and other sources of intelligence. Naval intelligence, the intelligence which mattered most during the phoney war, was treated completely separately from Army and Air Force intelligence, and afterwards Naval intelligence was handled mainly in Hut Four.

Even after the first changes had been made in the primitive scheme in Hut Three there was a contest for power within the hut. Personal differences counted for more in the contest than differing attitudes towards the collection and dissemination of intelligence. In the thick of it Humphreys was an excellent German linguist but no team player. He wanted to get his own way. He found this difficult to do if only because Saunders had a mind of his own. Nigel de Grey described the situation as 'an imbroglio of conflicting jealousies, intrigues and differing opinions'.

The immediate upshot of the contest between the first three of the contestants was that Travis moved the three of them out of Hut Three, and a small committee, which included Jones, was put in charge of it. This was not a workable solution, and in July 1942 Travis made Jones sole head, in the first instance for a trial period of three months. Just over a year after he took over H. S. Marchant was appointed as his deputy, and the pair stayed together for the rest of the war. I saw little of Jones, but liked Marchant, whom I knew less through his role in Hut Three than as a guiding spirit behind the revues in which members of many of the huts in BP took part, including myself as an occasional scriptwriter. Nonetheless, I read with interest some of the Watch Notes that Marchant, a man with a future, issued with the object of standardizing procedures in Hut Three and increasing accuracy, and I followed with interest his post-war career when, in the 1960s, he became ambassador first to Cuba, then to Tunisia.

There were several changes in Hut Three in March 1943, and indeed later, which directly impinged on my own work. Already there were specialized sections in Hut Three operating within what had become a settled framework. These included 3L, Sixta and the Central Party.

The setting up of 3L was designed to control the routing and distribution of all messages from their arrival in Hut Three until their emending and reporting had been completed. The emending and reporting were to be carried out in accordance with priorities determined by Jones and Marchant and laid down by 3L. I talked with members of Hut Three and of 3L about messages that they particularly wanted. We all appreciated the need for urgency, and as the war went on priorities were revised at least weekly at a meeting of members of Hut Six, 3L and Sixta.

Sixta, the section of Hut Six concerned with traffic analysis and the intelligence it carried, had evolved over the years before it got its name in November 1943. I had little notion of its extraordinary evolution when it moved into Block G. It then had more than twenty people working in it, including civilians and soldiers. It had started, nameless, in July 1940 after the collapse of France, as a one-man band stationed in London, not in BP. The one man, Edward Crankshaw, born in 1904, had as extraordinary a career as Sixta itself, culminating in his becoming head of it, if briefly, in 1943. He had never been to a university, but he wrote and spoke German extremely well, and he had unique German literary contacts.

He started intelligence work in London before the war in a building where, on a different floor, completely separate from him, the members of a log-reading group, known as the Central Party, were studying logs supplied by intercept stations. On his own initiative Crankshaw worked closely with them, and together they began to produce diagrams of the lines of German communications networks in France.

In October 1940 the Central Party moved out of blitzed London first to Harpenden and then to Beaumanor, and finally in May 1942 the log readers were moved from there to work in

Hut Six in BP. Meanwhile, Crankshaw had been seconded to the British Military Mission in Moscow, where it was his task to pass on officially information from BP to the Russians. From that vantage point in time and space he became a recognized authority on Russian history and language.

When I arrived in BP in the summer of 1943 Sixta was located in Block D where I was to work, and although it moved in November 1943, its relationship with Huts Six and Three remained close. Its weekly Sixta Summary was studied attentively in both huts. I myself considered it an integral part of Hut Six and, indeed, of BP, and I was shocked to learn years later that when it moved from Beaumanor there had been opposition inside BP to its members being drawn into the secrets of breaking Enigma. At the heart of Sixta was the Fusion Room, given its name at Beaumanor, now a room in BP where intelligence derived from traffic analysis was fused with intelligence derived from code-breaking.

Two of the people working in Sixta I came to know well in BP. Neil Webster, born in 1908, known at BP as Willie, was a major when I arrived; he had risen through the Central Party. Edward Rushworth (Rush), also a major, born in 1918, I have mentioned in a previous chapter. He had a stronger Yorkshire accent than I had. Sadly he died in 1975 just after BP's secrets were beginning to be revealed. This was only the beginning of a process. Revelation was to be as evolutionary a process as the structural reorganization of intelligence.

Rushworth loved maps, as I do, and in the Fusion Room there was a large map which I frequently examined as I did the cumulative index collated in Hut Three. It may well have been through the Fusion Room that I first developed my abiding belief in interdisciplinarity, a feature of 'the map of learning' which I drew up before the launching of the University of Sussex in 1961.

Coincidentally Rushworth's daughter Helen, born in 1946, was to be Director of the European Institute of Sussex University between 1998 and 2001.

The Fusion Room does not figure in Calvocoressi's *Top Secret Ultra*, where he approached issues of intelligence in a different way, pointing out that there was one 'immutable rule' in distributing it. Every message signalled to a particular command had to be reported to the superior headquarters of that command. Calvocoressi had the Air Force in mind, but what he wrote largely applied also to the Army. The Navy followed a different system through Hut Eight and Hut Four. Full integration, which had its advocates, was never achieved. There were other rules, of course, that were imposed in the interests of security, which was deemed paramount. The SLUs and SCUs watched over them. One was that nothing tangible relating to Ultra should be taken to any area where there was a risk of capture by the enemy. Despite how important this rule was for any intelligence service, it was found difficult to stick to in all circumstances.

Enigma was never referred to as such. Synonyms included 'Boniface', 'an unimpeachable source' and, simplest of all 'special stuff'. Martin Gilbert quotes the example of an Enigma decrypt which gave details, on 30 September 1942, of a German plan for naval action in the Caspian Sea as soon as German troops had crossed the Caucasus. Churchill summarized it and had it secretly transmitted by personal telegram to Stalin, bearing this 'comment':

> I have got the following information from the same source that I used to warn you of the impending attack on Russia a year and a half ago. I believe this source to be absolutely trustworthy. Pray let this be for your own eye.

Daily decrypts were important for both Churchill and Stalin. The latter used a totally different mode of communication through the spy John Cairncross, who sent an enormous amount of information to Moscow.

Earlier in 1942, the German non-Morse teleprinter cypher system known at BP as Tunny was broken. When I arrived in BP I quickly got to know many of the people engaged in Fish decyphering – their numbers were to grow – but I knew no more of the history and characteristics of Fish cyphers or of the building of great machines to try to break them than I did of the debates about fusion and integration. Part III of Hinsley and Stripp's *Codebreakers* is devoted to the story of Fish which starts, as does the story of Enigma, before the war and which livens up in the months before the Normandy landings of 1944. It is a story well worth telling even with the binary mathematics left out. It leads us into what we have come to call 'the digital age'.

It was in the second half of 1940 that unidentified non-Morse signals were picked up not in BP but by a Metropolitan Police unit at Denmark Hill. The first Tunny messages intercepted were on an experimental German Army link between Vienna and Athens. The Germans had used a Lorenz Schlüsselzusatz cypher machine, SZ40. There was another somewhat heavier teleprinter encyphering system, T52, the Siemens und Halske Geheimschreiber, used mainly by the Luftwaffe, and called Sturgeon in BP. But it was on Tunny, used mainly by the Army, not on Sturgeon, that BP concentrated. Its breaking complemented all the work being carried out on breaking Enigma. German Army Enigma keys, which were used mainly at command level, were less easy to break than Luftwaffe keys, whereas Tunny was used mainly for communication higher up between Berlin and the commanders-in-chief of army groups and of armies. It threw light on strategy.

In July 1942 a section under Major Ralph Tester, formally working in Tiltman's military section, was directed to deal with Tunny. It became known as the Testery, one of the few sections in BP to be named after a person working there. Thirty-nine-year-old Tester, by civilian profession an accountant, had only recently made his way to BP from the BBC's monitoring section at Caversham. He had excellent German. The success of his work at BP depended on Post Office cooperation. A farm at Knockholt, near Sevenoaks in Kent, was acquired as an intercept site, and Frank Morrell, a Dollis Hill researcher, produced a machine which employed standard Post Office relays and contact switches to simulate the row of wheels of the Lorenz SZ40. Knockholt, staffed mainly by members of the ATS, came into operation in mid-1942. It was an ambitious venture. There were six dedicated teleprinter lines, used in pairs between Knockholt and BP.

Throughout 1942 work on the Tunny material had to be done entirely by hand, with the very clever young mathematicians working on it having to rely to a considerable extent on various German operators' mistakes. The notion of a machine to assist and, above all, to speed up their efforts became obvious. It was a mathematics lecturer from Manchester University, Max(well) Newman, born in 1897, the son of a German immigrant, who thought out a way to build one, and when he informed Travis of what funds he needed to do it Travis encouraged him as warmly and as speedily as he had encouraged Turing and Welchman when they approached him about the funding of bombe building. Was it a coincidence that Newman had taught Turing at Cambridge?

A new section called the Newmanry, which like the Testery was named after its leader, was now created. Newman, a highly disciplined organizer, was given valuable assistance by Donald

Michie, already identified, who had worked in the Testery and showed a remarkable aptitude for probability statistics and for Boolean logic, which were the methods employed. Another valuable assistant was I. J. (Jack) Good, a Cambridge mathematician. Newman also needed help from outside and travelled to Malvern to ask C. E. Wynn-Williams, a former Cambridge physics don, who was working at the Telecommunications Research Establishment, to design a machine that would depend on electronics, a new word and a new technology. It had a less memorable name than bombe, being called 'Robinson'. Newman and Wynn-Williams observed that the name of the machine drew on satire, not science. They had Heath Robinson in mind.

There was a bolder name to come, Colossus, which owed most to the engineer Tom (Tommy) Flowers, who had no Cambridge, or indeed any university, connections. He had joined the Telephone Branch of the Post Office in 1926, and six years later he had moved over to its Research Branch at Dollis Hill. By the time war was declared Flowers had established through his experiments that electronic valves could be effectively employed in high-speed digital switching. A huge number of valves was needed to build the machine. The first prototype Colossus, delivered to BP on 18 January 1944, was equipped with friction-driven tapes, electronic wheels and approximately 1,600 valves and operated at 5,000 characters per second. Later models were to employ far more valves and even more greatly to boost the speed. By May 1945 there were to be no fewer than ten Colossi in operation in BP.

Before the arrival of the prototype, which was received it is said with 'incredulity' in BP, teams in the Testery and the Newmanry were breaking around 250 Fish messages a month, but working under 'terrific pressure' they never found their task easy. As in the case of Enigma it was the 'bad habits' of operators which enabled the cypher to be broken: Bream, the link between Berlin and Rome, and Jellyfish, the link between Berlin and Paris, sometimes sent out identical messages. The good news for the people working on Fish was that on 25 May, a few days before the Allied landings in Normandy, it had been decided to go ahead with building a new Block H which would house six Colossi. A Mark II Colossus entered service on 2 June 1944.

During the middle months of 1944 there was a burst in the volume of Fish traffic received in BP, the fortunes of war influencing the pattern. The German operators of Bream had had to leave Rome for a transmitting point near Florence, and after D-Day the operators of Jellyfish had to leave Paris.

## Chapter 5

# Two Camps – and More

I had got used to being billeted in Bedford and travelling to and from there by train and by every variety of BP coach. Now, when the Shenley Road Military Camp was opened in January 1944, all BP men and women in military uniform, officers, warrant officers, NCOs – there were no male privates – had to leave their billets and move into real huts that bore no resemblance to the huts inside the Park. Some of our billets had been comfortable, some, like mine, friendly and clean. I left Bower Street in Bedford with happy memories; I would never have chosen to live there, however, I was just sent.

Many civilians working in BP felt very unhappy about their billets. Lighting was one of their main complaints. Bathrooms and inside toilets could not be taken for granted. Food, when provided, could be good or bad. 'I was billeted in Milton Keynes village with the vicar and his wife', one satisfied young woman wrote, 'heavenly house and heaps of food.'

The Shenley Road Military Camp was built because the number of men and women in uniform was rising sharply and the number of civilian billets available to take them in was not increasing. Who planned the Camp, as it came to be called, or who took the decision to build it we never knew at the time. Nor indeed, in 1943, when builders, carpenters, plumbers and electricians were hard at work on the site, did we know what was going on. I cannot remember any rumours in circulation. We sensed, however, that our billeting days were almost over.

I did know that throughout the war the administration of BP itself was controlled by Commander Bradshaw, the senior naval officer at BP, whom you had to know if you wanted to get things done. Fletcher said of him that he worked on the principle of meeting any request he was unsure of with 'a stream of naval abuse'. If, however, the person making the request stayed firm and resolved he would usually give it his approval.

We moved to the Camp, which was apparently first discussed a year earlier, in the worst kind of wintry weather. The site was muddy. The coke stoves were unlit. The electricians' work was incomplete. Before you could make your bed you had to fill your palliasses for yourself with straw from a building separate from that of the quartermaster who had supplied you with blankets. Most of us had had experiences of palliasses before. The ATS were supplied with three square palliasses for each wooden bed.

They were supposed to sleep sixteen to eighteen in a hut, but at first some of the huts were seriously overcrowded. A poem by ATS Sergeant M. C. Knowles caught the mood:

> Sing ho! for the lumps, the creases and bumps,
> Sing hey! for the Senior Commander.
> We'd all give our souls for the little tin bowls
> We use to perform our ablutions.
> We go off our heads for our nice wooden beds
> A comfort to frail constitutions.

The name of the ATS Senior Commandant was unknown to the ATS working at BP when they arrived at the Camp, but they very soon found it out. Mrs Kemp inspired a satire, *Mein Kemp*:

Until the war for freedom's won,
Their freedom will get littler
For in this camp I'll have you know –
I am not Kemp but Hitler.

It was more difficult to complain to her than it had been to complain to a Billeting Officer.

Male soldiers entering the Camp do not seem to have resorted to poetry, but they were equally ignorant when they arrived at Shenley Road who their Officer in Command of Troops, the commandant of the main camp, would be. It was one of BP's many secrets. In this case, however, it very quickly ceased to be one. Lieutenant Colonel Fillingham of the Durham Light Infantry was initially unknown to everyone except to the DLI privates who dealt with 'amenities', at first an ironic term, inside the Camp. He had previously been in command of a young soldiers' battalion of the DLI.

Almost at once Fillingham established a formidable reputation with us all. There were as many stories about him as there were about the personalities inside the Park. For him, most of us were like young soldiers anywhere. Yet Fillingham became as well known to me personally as any military officer inside BP except for the brilliant cryptographer John Tiltman, born in 1894, who for all his reputation as a man apart seemed to take a personal interest in my welfare and prospects from the day of my arrival in BP. Fillingham was never allowed to enter the Park, but within the Camp his word was law, and, if he liked you, as he luckily liked me, he would take as lively a personal interest in your career as a soldier as Tiltman did in your career as a cryptographer in uniform.

I cannot clearly remember Fillingham's regimental sergeant major, RSM Conners, not of the DLI but of the Black Watch, which my future brother-in-law had joined. Conners may have had more warrant officers class I in his mess than any other RSM in the country. He was said to have been offered a commission, but he had preferred to stay a warrant officer. Few of his warrant officers had had the choice. To complete the picture, no other commandant could have had more sergeants and warrant officers sleeping in the huts of his camp than Fillingham had.

The ATS had more complaints about their huts than I had. To me most of them were more comfortable than the old huts in the Park. One ATS NCO claimed that they were erected so speedily that 'a roof blew right off in a high wind'. Another complained that acrid smells from a primitive iron stove forced her to pick up her bed and sleep outside in pouring rain – on her ground sheet and under her gas cape.

There would be little rest in the camp for people working on night shift. Indeed, Camp routines were so different from BP routines that what would have been acceptable within most other army camps grated in Shenley Road. I was lucky in having a room to myself where I kept a typewriter and even a small library. Warrant officers fared relatively well. The warrant officer I knew best was John Kirby who was with me in Hut Six, though not working with me in the Watch. Quiet and reserved, but not lacking in wit, he played no bigger a part in the Camp than he did in the Park. At the end of the war he was to become librarian of the History Faculty Library in Oxford. My closest friend in the Camp was Frank Newte, who in civilian life was a lecturer at Lampeter. Jimmy Thirsk, who was a librarian before and after the war, remembered Newte when he was a corporal at Beaumanor, 'gentle and erudite'.

In the mess he was not always gentle. I argued about politics with him at immense length – and passionately. He was the most right-wing friend that I have ever had. Our good relations only just survived the Labour victory at the general election of 1945. He thought that a country that had thrown out Churchill was not worth living in. I was saved only because he thought that my getting a fellowship at Oxford would take me straight into Paradise.

Most of the warrant officers and sergeants in BP shared my views, not his. Among them was Eric Plant, who had also known Newte at Beaumanor. What I most enjoyed in the mess was playing ping-pong, as we all called it, with him and with others. I also loved talking about music with another friend of mine, Herbert Murrill. He invited the composer Edmund Rubbra, who held a fellowship in my future Oxford college, to give a concert in the mess. Rubbra was to be a colleague of mine in Worcester College after the war.

It seemed to me that in many ways the most talented, if also the most eccentric, soldier in the mess was Stuart Rigold, a gifted cartoonist, whose inability to march made him a cartoon character in his own right. I have no idea what he did inside BP. In the Camp we had our historian as well as our cartoonist. Alfred Sugar, a log-reader in the Park, was to publish after the war an annual news circular which tried to remain up-to-date in describing what old members of the sergeants' mess were doing. Its title was *The Nosey Parker, with which is incorporated Military Training Excuse Note, Chairborne Chronicle, Penpushers' Friend, Pram-pushers' Post, Four-fifty-eight Flyer, Guardroom Gazette and the Blancoist*. There were echoes of the Intelligence Corps depot in the last of these. The adjutant there had insisted on our using a particularly nasty variety of blanco, and Sugar had shared my other unpleasant experiences while living there. We talked about them often in the Camp. *The Nosey*

*Parker* survived until October 1957, and Alfred himself lived to be a hundred. As far as I know, he was BP's only centenarian to date. He died in 2007.

There were more soldiers in the camp who were single than there were married men, and it was natural, therefore, that Sugar, in his circular was more informative about marriages and births and deaths than he was about careers. I did not learn, therefore, until much later that Rigold, who died in 1980, had been made Principal Inspector of Ancient Monuments and Public Buildings just before he died. I followed with interest what happened to Peter Benenson, founder of Amnesty, who worked in the Testery, and used to give excellent parties outside both Camp and Park. They were remarkable for their size and for the diversity of people attending them.

It was there that I met, for example, Donald Michie, two years younger than myself, who was a friend of Turing and who was deeply involved in the breaking of Tunny and the exploitation of Colossus. In 1952 he was to marry Ann McLaren who during the war worked with me in Hut Six. She was highly intelligent.

The intellectual and social mix of the Camp contrasted markedly with the mix in Hut Six. I felt at the time, maybe wrongly, that there were no women in the Camp who were comparable in brainpower with Ann or in beauty with Janet Muir and Shiela Dunlop, favourites of Milner-Barry. The girls I liked most in Hut Six included a significant proportion of girls from Scotland who were not only attractive but clever. What diaries I kept at the time focused on them. Cryptography was taboo. The gender mix in the Park was totally unlike the gender mix in Cambridge where, even in 1941 with many male undergraduates in the forces, women were in a minority. A bigger group of women from Oxford, with a similar gender pattern to Cambridge, were arriving in BP between 1943 and 1945. It was then, I believe, that BP seemed most like a university. The Camp never did.

There was an underclass of privates in the Camp engaged in general duties; they were largely drawn from infantry regiments. I was more conscious of them than I was of all the people in the Park who had nothing at all to do with code-breaking but carried out all the necessary menial tasks. There were no fewer than 152 'house staff' in 1945, cleaners, handymen and watchmen. Military officers in the Camp had orderlies, of course, and that, not social background or individual ability, distinguished them from warrant officers and sergeants. When one of them, a young 2nd lieutenant, tried to pull his rank on me, telling RSM Conners on a room inspection that my blankets were not properly folded and that I should be put on a charge, the RSM warned him that it would be stupid to do so and that our Commandant would not approve. Later he tried to get into my college in Oxford.

I was a pretty high-profile member of the sergeants' mess, and it was an amusing example of Fillingham's trust in me that I was asked to assume the role of the Princess Royal in rehearsals preceding her visit to the Camp and, I believe, the Park. That was a rare double. It was fun when Fillingham insisted that I should be addressed as 'Ma'am' during the rehearsals. Fillingham was unpopular when he introduced early morning PT, physical training. I did not resent it. From fragmentary diaries I find that I 'did' PT more often than I recall.

There seemed to be a more unattractive atmosphere in BP's second camp, the RAF camp in Church Green Road, built in fields north-west of the Park, which opened after Shenley Road. There was a military sentry there at the gates carrying a rifle and calling out 'Halt. Who goes there?' He intimidated RAF personnel working in the camp as much as people like myself, particularly warrant officers from the Shenley Road Camp. There were around 200 buildings in Church Green Road which were sometimes described as camps, not camp. The adjective 'camp' carried no weight in BP.

Gwen Watkins has described the WAAF camp vividly in her book *Cracking the Luftwaffe Codes*. The menial jobs both in the women's RAF camp and in the men's, like disposing of rubbish or cleaning the ablutions (a word I learnt at Bletchley), were carried out by ACHs, Aircraft Hands, 'the lowest of all Air Force trades', who nonetheless included musicians who were called upon to play selections from *The Desert Song* and *Rose Marie* when the Camp Commandant, whom she does not name, entertained visitors, a task that Fillingham also liked to do but with more sense in the Shenley Road Camp.

All ranks in both camps were required to wear uniform at all times, never a requirement inside the Park, and saluting was obligatory. Gwen also noted that in the RAF camp the male huts were rigidly separated from the female huts. Nevertheless, like most of the WAAFs, she had experience of other RAF camps and believed that in Church Green Camp there were compensations. You did not have to spend a large part of the day travelling to billets; I was consoled by that too. You might, if you tried, live in a hut – she picked out Male Hut 54 – which you shared with people who worked with you in the Camp or that you knew and liked. You did not just sleep in the huts. 'Hut fifty-four was the scene of very varied activities. Debates, discussions, gramophone recitals, games of hockey with a rolled-up sock and anything that came to hand as a stick.'

Gwen's concluding thoughts were that, although some WAAFs hated the Camp all the time, she did not. She compared her reactions with those of WAAF Ann Lavell, who worked closely inside BP with Josh Cooper. Ann disliked everything in the Camp from the huts to the RAF officers in charge of 'discipline'; they found 'every way of encroaching on free time that petty tyranny could suggest'. Gwen found life in the Camp 'bustling'; she made friends with people she would have otherwise never met. She was aware of other RAF camps which were worse, as was BP's out-station Chicksands, where WAAFs lived in Nissen huts and shared bathing facilities. Before improvements were made, they worked on the site in a 'watch room' high up in the ancient priory, where interception was disturbed by bats breaking loose from a vaulted ceiling. Most WAAFs serving in BP were dealing with wireless, and the wireless room was staffed entirely by them except for two male RAF technicians. Most of the RAF officers dealing with wireless inside BP and in its out-stations were former employees of Cable and Wireless, which for decades had served as an adjunct to the British intelligence system. They were civilians temporarily in uniform.

Naval officers often came from a different social background from RAF officers and they and the Wrens had no camp of their own at BP. Nevertheless, in the requisitioned premises taken over for Wrens, camp-like rules, disguised in naval nomenclature, prevailed. In March 1941 there were only the eight Wrens working on bombes in BP; by 1945 there were 1,676 of them located in six different places. All the naval personnel were said to belong to HMS *Pembroke*, and wherever they lived their living-quarters were called forecastles, their dormitories cabins and the areas in front of their premises the quarterdeck. They were under the authority of a Chief Officer whom they had to salute.

'Wrenery' premises were often historic houses, the most grand of which, Woburn, home of the idiosyncratic Duke of Bedford, was set in an ancient deer park. When BP Wrens arrived at

Woburn, some well after midnight, they had to wipe their feet in disinfectant straw in order to protect the deer against infectious disease. Inside their cabins at Woburn the drainage systems sometimes failed and the water was contaminated. As a result, water had to be imported from BP.

As I have noted, various other groups of intelligence personnel worked and lived at Woburn, and the Wrens, who were envied by ATS and WAAFs for the superiority of their lot, actually lived in the least attractive premises in Woburn Park itself. Those other Wrens, the minority, who were working with bombes in BP's outstations, both lived and worked in less desirable premises. In historic houses like Gayhurst Manor, where Sir Francis Drake was said to have lived, there were Wrens who considered their conditions were intolerable. Mice abounded and swallows flew in and out through broken windows. In the village of Adstock, where Travis lived throughout the war, food was sent over to the Wrens living there from BP in a large container.

Apart from my own Camp and Woburn, the BP camp that I knew best was the American Camp at Little Brickhill. To me it was a wonderful place, both civilized and comfortable. I went there often, appreciating both the company and the food. I was always welcome. I have more photographs of myself there than of anywhere else in BP, and I have none of Shenley Road. There were two people living at Little Brickhill whom I worked with in the Hut Six Watch. Captain Bill Bundy and Lieutenant Lew Smadbeck – but the people I saw most when I visited the American Camp were working in BP not in the Hut Six Watch but in other sections of Hut Six or Hut Three. The cleverest of them was reputed to be Art Levenson.

The ones I knew best were historians with whom I kept in touch after the war, among them LeRoy Fisher, an historian of the

American Civil War who plied me with books on the subject, and Mat Simon, an economic historian who introduced me to branches of economic history and its methodology that I had never studied at Cambridge. Rank mattered no more in the American Camp than it did in Hut Six. Yet promotion was always celebrated. I remember well Bill Bijur's promotion to the rank of lieutenant. He lavishly distributed champagne and cigars all round.

Rank certainly did not matter in the many romances between Americans and British girls inside and outside BP. I heard more of one American romance than any other. My best American friend in the Camp was a good-looking Harvard graduate, Frank Stanton, who composed music of the kind that the big bands liked, and in BP he fell in love with and married a very attractive girl called Rosemary (Romi) who went to America with him when the war ended. If Fisher introduced me to American colleges and universities very different from Yale, like the Oklahoma College of Agriculture and Technology and Austin, Texas, Frank introduced me to Broadway and later to Nashville, where he and his family subsequently went to live. By then tastes in music had changed, and Frank's fortunes suffered in consequence. Big bands were 'out' or on their way out: 'country and western' was in. So was boogie-woogie, which one of my fellow signalmen at Catterick Camp had played superbly on any camp or pub piano to which he was given access. Frank could not stand either.

Through my relationship with Frank I eventually learned as much about American music as I learned about American food and drink at the Camp. At Little Brickhill I ate my first avocados, tasted my first American coffee, infinitely superior to the coffee we drank in Hut Six or at Shenley Road, and drank my first bourbon and my first dry martini. I was never the same again. When the Americans first arrived in BP the drink that they were offered was very poor (British?) sherry. I noted that had it been good sherry that would have been a truly Oxbridge gesture. Fortunately neither Bundy nor his men objected to drinking British beer. There was a beer hut inside BP, although the beer served there was not as good as the beer served outside in the pubs of Bletchley village.

These reflections lead me naturally into my next chapter which is broadly concerned with what other writers have called 'the culture of Bletchley Park'. However, I knew then – and I know better now – that the word culture should always be used in the plural. It was in Birmingham University and in the Open University that the study of popular culture came into its own.

## Chapter 6

# Ways of Escape

However many cultures there were in BP and in Bletchley – and I shall return to them in the last part of this chapter – most young BPites were keen to escape from time to time from the Park. The chief memory of BP for one young girl, Mary Seymour (née Hambro), who arrived in Hut Six in 1942 as a Foreign Office clerk grade III and who worked in it for nearly a year before moving to Japanese intelligence in London, was rushing down the path to the railway station after the 9 to 4 shift to catch a train to London. She enjoyed 'partying with friends on leave or who worked in London' and returned to Bletchley on the milk train the following morning in time for the 9 o'clock shift. So did many debs. The one deb who has said and written most about BP debs since 1945 was the Honourable Sarah Baring. She was frequently photographed by Cecil Beaton.

Age mattered more inside BP than social origins, and rushing up to London is also one of my own chief recollections, as it must be for many other BPites. Many of the people in the crowded trains travelling to Euston from the north must have been surprised at Bletchley station to see large numbers of soldiers of all ranks wearing Intelligence Corps shoulder flashes. Within the railway station the forces canteen on the station was the most democratic institution in Britain. All ranks used it, and any Military Police who were around kept out of the way. Military

Police were conspicuous at Euston, however, which still linked the historic station with central London through its great Doric arch, to be pulled down amid controversy in 1961.

Some of the people working in BP had never been to peacetime London, but for them, as for those who knew London already, the lure of the sand-bagged wartime city was always strong. The metropolis contrasted sharply with Bletchley, which until 1914 had usually been described as a hamlet and before 1939 at best as a small nondescript town. One future secretary of the Victorian Society, Jane Fawcett, described it as a 'dump', and Nikolaus Pevsner totally left it out of his series *The Buildings of England*, the first volume of which was published in 1951; it was one of those places in England which he did not think worthy of a visit.

Non-Londoners, whatever they thought of Bletchley, soon realized that there were many different areas in London, including places as different as Soho and Kensington, each with distinctive features, and that, in particular, there was as sharp a distinction between west and east as there was between England's north and south. The east had been badly bombed during the Blitz of 1940 and there were gaps in the west too where willowherb was picking its way through the ruins. Once arrived in London BPites quickly got used to crowded underground stations and equally crowded underground trains.

Whatever the rubble and the mess, metropolitan theatres, cinemas and concerts beckoned, and theatre and concert tickets were cheap. There were even a few kiosks where members of the forces, if they queued, could get them free. Apart from entertainment food was a preoccupation on visits from Bletchley to London. BPites learned quickly how to choose restaurants, many of them far away from Euston. Prices of restaurant meals everywhere were rigorously controlled, with an upper price limit, but there was considerable variety in the fare on offer. My favourite restaurant in Soho was a Hungarian establishment in Dean Street which has sadly now disappeared. It was enterprising and welcoming, and its menus always included Hungarian dishes which, like some of the American dishes in their Little Brickhill Camp, I had never tasted before. Other favourite BP restaurants were said to be Harrods, Simpson's, Liberty's and The Mirabelle. I occasionally travelled outside this charmed circle and spent a weekend with an old undergraduate friend of mine, James Roe, who was a curate south of the river in Bermondsey.

Those of us who arrived in BP a little later than Mary Hambro did not care much about the dangers either of 'doodle bugs', V1s, buzzing before they landed, or of V2s which gave no indication as they approached of the place where they would explode. This seems surprising now. In Hut Six in our work many of us learned as much about rockets as the Germans who launched them. Named by Hitler reprisal weapons, *Vergeltungswaffen*, they will figure again in Chapter 7 of this book. Bletchley itself was outside the range of both V1s and V2s.

Fortunately there were ways of escape, admittedly limited, in the Bletchley area itself. The countryside around Bletchley was covered with brickworks and tall brick chimneys, but in springtime it could look attractive. I had never seen blackthorn before. Cycling was popular, and there was no shortage of places to keep bikes in BP. There were even a few attractive pubs in the countryside, not too far away from Bletchley, like what one BPite called 'a nice little pub at Pottersbury', where the landlady kept back little titbits for girls from BP, and the Galleon Inn, formerly called The Locomotive, in Old Wolverton, overlooking the Grand Junction Canal. I went to a boisterous and protracted party there to celebrate the winning of the war in Europe.

The names Galleon and Grand Junction Canal recall the pre-motorway forms of transport which had made the Bletchley area what it was with the railways. New Wolverton, as much of a railway town as Crewe, was constructed on a grid pattern; it still had a huge tram carrying a hundred people at a time to and from 'the Works' where there were 4,000 employees building and repairing trains. There was also a Wolverton hooter announcing that it was time to get off to work. Many BPites were billeted in Wolverton. Many more went to the cinema there. Sometimes they were surprised by the hospitality they received, more often, perhaps, disappointed. Beyond the railway area was Newport Pagnell. It had an attraction of its own.

There were many railways around Bletchley as well as the Euston line which linked it with London, Rugby, Northampton and the north. Some trains went to Banbury and Bicester, both of them then railway junctions. There was also an east–west line linking Oxford and Cambridge, which I and many other people at BP used more often than the Euston line. Bedford, where many BPites were billeted, was on the way to Cambridge. It was at the centre of its own very different landscape from that of Bletchley. One of my favourite outings was to Olney, an attractive place on the river, the home of the poet William Cowper and the anti-slavery campaigner John Newton.

An interesting and highly informative book on railways around Bletchley, *The Town of Trains* (1980), written by a locomotive driver, A. L. (Sam) Grigg, had an introduction by Sir Peter Parker, then chairman of nationalized British Rail, but Grigg was so restrained by continuing secrecy rules that he made only the briefest references to the wartime golden age of Bletchley. Indeed, he devoted only one brief paragraph to the wartime existence of BP as a communications and intelligence centre:

Several hundreds of people did secret work in the grounds [of Bletchley Park] and their dispersal for living accommodation meant a regular daily train to and from Bedford, appropriately named 'The Whitehall'. It was a short walk from Bletchley Station through the wicket gate opposite to the Park and the Coffee Nob, as the Coffee Tavern was affectionately known, became a popular place.

In this paragraph Grigg was no more reliable than Winterbotham. The hundreds in his brief paragraph should have been thousands, and his names beg questions. I never heard the train to Bedford described as the Whitehall or the Coffee Tavern called the Coffee Nob, and I associated the wicket gate more with *Pilgrim's Progress* than with BP. To me it would have been more relevant if *The Town of Trains* had mentioned all the BP people who were then billeted in railwaymen's cottages, but I was delighted by his reference to Mrs Briggs, 49 Duncombe Street, who billeted railway chiefs from Crewe in Bletchley before the war. One of the first wartime BPites billeted in Bletchley was John Herivel, who in the solitude of his Bletchley billet, situated conveniently near to the station and the Park on a hill sloping down from the Park to the railway bridge, hit upon the idea of the Herivel Tip.

Inside Hut Six Herivel's colleague John Manisty was an authority on every railway line in the country and its timetable, and he provided me and other people working in the Hut, soldiers and civilians, with invaluable information on how best to get home on leave. It must have taken up a lot of his time. By 1945 he knew as much about trains through to Keighley as I did. None of them was direct. He also knew about railways in very remote parts of Scotland. Sheila Lawn testifies to this. One complication in his reckoning was that most trains, except those from Euston to Bletchley, did not arrive in Bletchley at the allotted time. Troop trains and trains carrying war materials were understandably given priority. Throughout the whole of the war soldiers could be seen on Bletchley platform waiting for the 5 a.m. to Bicester, where there was a big new ordnance depot.

The blackout made life on most un-named railway stations as uneasy, even as precarious, as blackout on the trains themselves. Yet there was as great a diversity in the services offered by railway stations near Bletchley as there was in their architecture. Bletchley station, rebuilt in 1881, had Doric arches. On Verney Junction, which seemed as remote as any station could be, there was a book-stall. There were weekly excursions to London. Visitors coming to see relatives working at BP sometimes chose Bedford or Leighton Buzzard as the places to meet.

Grigg's book ends with two photographs of Bletchley Station, one showing a sad deterioration in style after the war. Steam gave way to diesel and diesel to electrification, and all the stations on the Oxbridge line and other local lines, familiar to BPites during the war, were closed before 1959 when the line ceased to take passengers. Only the line to Bedford remained.

Grigg had little to say about what went on in the hamlets, villages and small towns behind his railway stations. There were, in fact, many railway pubs and pubs which depended on railway traffic. Among them was the Shoulder of Mutton, where Hugh Alexander, Stuart Milner-Barry, James Passant and for a time Gordon Welchman lived, the first two until the end of the war. The landlady was unusual in providing occasional food for parties. Her merits were hailed.

Elsewhere in Bletchley there was little pub food and not much interesting pub furniture. Yet, while there was a shortage of spirits in the pubs, none of them ever seemed to run out of beer. For regular customers the pub landlords kept many drinks locked away from the general public. There was little mixing between railwaymen, who played games like darts, shuffleboard, shove ha'penny and dominoes, and BPites. Some 'hostelries' were very much railwaymen's pubs, and I do not remember seeing anyone playing chess in any pub. Three pubs with obviously erudite customers were the Duncombe Arms in Great Brickhill and the Cock and the Bull, two old stabling inns in Stony Stratford. It was reputed that a few of their customers spoke classical Greek to each other over their beer.

There were other aspects of railway culture in Bletchley, like gambling, which seldom drew in BPites. Nevertheless, I knew a few BPites who patronized Bletchley bookies, some of whom travelled into Bletchley from outside. I was aware that many railwaymen considered gambling to be immoral and refused all 'strong drink'. Bible classes were a feature of *their* culture, which rested less on respectability than on mutual self-help. I do not know who ran the local brass band and I cannot remember if there was a Salvation Army. I knew at first hand the local Co-op, created by railway families, which had a tailoring department, much used by soldiers, and a laundry. There were many civilians who had never been Co-op customers before working in BP. If you did not have a dividend number, then a universal feature of Co-operative stores, you could use a dividend number of the Aid to Russia Fund, chaired by Mrs Churchill, on whom Stalin conferred the Red Banner of Labour. Many of us hoped that she would pay a visit to BP.

There were two cinemas in Bletchley village, one of them, the Odeon, converted from a former non-conformist chapel. There were cinemas in other villages, however, not only at Wolverton but at Fenny Stratford. My diary records my impressions of some of the films I saw, but I did not describe in it the queues that often stood outside waiting for the next show. With high wartime cinema attendances these were a familiar sight. There was a film society in the Park, however, which showed foreign as well as British films and documentaries. Among the films I saw was the Post Office's *Night Mail*, which must have had a distinctive appeal to railwaymen. In London I preferred the theatre to the cinema, and I got to know some of London's theatres quite well.

Musical concerts were given in the Camp as well as in the Park, and in the Corn Exchange in Bedford. In the Park the first concerts early in the war were held in what had come to be called the main lounge of the Mansion. Late in the war an assembly hall was built just outside the Park where larger concerts were arranged. Among the musicians who came to BP to take part in them were Myra Hess and Peter Pears. What was happening in the Park was completely secret to them. The Bletchley Recreation Club met many demands, and its first president, L. P. Wilkinson, listed its activities for Commander Bradshaw; they included plays, revues and pantomimes, performed by a BP drama group, later called the Dramatic Club, presided over by Shaun Wylie, which included some professional actors. I have kept my BRC card. I was allowed to pay for it in instalments.

Most of these activities would not have taken place in Bletchley had not BP been located there, and it was a testimony to the local role of BP, whatever occasional misunderstandings there might have been, that at the end of the war the local newspaper the *Bletchley Gazette* regretted that the Bletchley Park Drama Group was producing its last play. In its early days the members of the group had 'rushed about the countryside' in BP transport vehicles 'giving entertainments in conjunction with the musical societies in village halls'. 'The Group was indebted', the *Gazette* concluded, 'to the people and particularly to the traders of Bletchley who have always given lots of support.'

In my next chapter I turn to the end of the war. I am not sure, however, whether I chose the right title for this chapter was right 'Ways of Escape'. Many people in BP liked to work hard. Some kept themselves very much to themselves. Their pursuits were very much private pursuits. For every play performed there were a dozen play readings. Private reading was a daily occupation for many people who never discussed what they were reading with others. You could be almost sure of seeing someone else from BP in Heffers bookshop in Cambridge or Blackwells in Oxford. Writing poetry was more common in BP than in any other place where I have ever lived. We all knew that what we were doing would not go on for ever, but none of us knew quite what was going to happen next.

## Chapter 7

# The End of the War

If D-Day was the climax of my BP experience, as I claimed in an earlier chapter, I still had much to learn at BP both as a cryptographer and as an historian after 6 June 1944. The news rushed along. The liberation of Paris, Brussels, Strasbourg and Antwerp were highlights in the Allied campaign in the West that took us from Normandy to Germany itself. On 20 July 1944 came the failure of the German Army plot to blow up Hitler and the military purge that followed. On 20 August 1944 the Russians launched a massive offensive in the southern part of the Eastern Front and swept into the Balkans. In September the Allies in Italy breached the Gothic Line and crossed the Rubicon. On 14 October Rommel obeyed orders to commit suicide. In the same month Tito's Partisans moved into Belgrade and Dubrovnik, and British forces landed in Greece and entered Athens. In November General Slim, leading the fight in Burma, sent his troops across the Chindwin in three places. At last, it seemed, we were moving forwards towards victory, if not always in the way that General Eisenhower wished, while the Russians were advancing triumphantly on all fronts. We sometimes called them theatres.

It was extraordinary to be able to follow what was happening in the east, west and in the south from the German Enigma sources that we were breaking in the Watch. We were aware that we were providing Hut Three with an immense amount of information about what was happening, though we knew it was not always correct or easy to interpret. I felt that I was participating in the making of history not merely – the right adverb in our circumstances – watching it.

That history was not always agreeable to contemplate. We were learning all the time of the horrors of the Nazi regime, but were struck by the refusal of most Germans to smash it. After Warsaw was devastated when the rising there was ruthlessly put down Hitler called up all Germans between the ages of sixteen and sixty to fight in the Volkssturm. It was dispiriting too to learn of our set-back at Arnhem in September 1944, when Allied troops were forced to evacuate a Rhine bridgehead, and even more so to follow the German offensive across the lightly defended Ardennes area of Belgium which started on 16 December.

Theirs was a surprise attack, and at this late stage of the war I learned far more about what was going on from my work in Hut Six than the general public was allowed to know in the shape of news. I knew – and know – little about the terrain of the Ardennes, but I knew a lot – and since the war have got to know far more – about the Germans' target destination, the city of Antwerp across the River Meuse, for us an essential port of supply. It was one of Europe's great cities of history, as was the city of Ravenna in Italy, which by a coincidence rather than a convergence the British Eighth Army captured on the day before the German Ardennes offensive began.

I wish that I had been able to keep a diary of the course of the German offensive, carried out by fourteen infantry and seven Panzer divisions under Field Marshal von Rundstedt, as we saw it in BP at the time. My own pocket diary is entirely personal. I remember mainly that the offensive took us by surprise. There had been a period of radio silence before it began. There had also been successful German deception surrounding the location of the attack, not as dramatic as Allied deception had been before D-Day but perhaps more effective.

There was criticism from on high, which I did not hear much of at the time, of the failures of Allied intelligence. In earlier campaigns BP had supplied detailed information derived from Enigma on German deployment and, indeed, on timing. Hut Three set up an enquiry of its own after the offensive had failed. F. L. Lucas and Peter Calvocoressi wrote a report, which soon disappeared from view, showing that, through traffic analysis as well as Enigma, evidence had been collected and passed on about movements of aircraft from the Russian Front to the Ardennes and transport of other forces by rail to the Ardennes. 'We could not give a precise date or the point of attack', Calvocoressi wrote later, 'but we did show that a substantial and offensive operation was in the wind.'

What determined the fate of Hitler's gamble, as it came to be seen, and which was described by Calvocoressi as fundamental to its failure, was not intelligence but weather. The Germans had called the offensive Operation Herbstnebel (Autumn Mist). In fact, they were to encounter not autumn mist but winter snow, for they struck in the worst Belgian winter in living memory. Mobile warfare was difficult in such conditions; the Panzer divisions had to move more slowly than they expected. Yet the weather affected the Allies as much as the Germans. Allied air forces were themselves immobilized until Christmas Day.

I was on night duty in the Watch on Christmas Eve. By then Rundstedt had reached the limit of his resources, and the 'Battle of the Bulge', as it was quickly called, ended with German failure on 25 January 1945. The very last German offensive of the war in the West, in the Saar region of Alsace, launched on New Year's

Day, failed also. I find it difficult to separate what I knew at BP about the Ardennes or Saar campaigns from what I have read about them since. What I did know then was that I was busier in BP in January and February 1945 than I had ever been before and that I felt thoroughly at home in the Watch.

I was also working in the Watch on Monday 7 May, my birthday, when I received and passed on to Hut Three a message in clear from Grand Admiral Dönitz, Commander-in-Chief of the German Navy and Hitler's successor, saying that Germany had surrendered unconditionally. This was one of many messages in clear received in Hut Six during the last days of the war. I felt that I was participating in history as I received it and passed it on with a mingled sense of excitement and relief. I did not know that three days earlier Dönitz had been present at a meeting in Flensburg, his new headquarters, attended by his Foreign Minister, Schwerin von Krosigk, and General Jodl, representing the high command, at which they had agreed (in face of opposition) on unconditional surrender. I did know, however, that on the same day Dönitz ordered an end to the U-boat war which he had fought relentlessly. The following day he abandoned plans for a German underground resistance movement brought into being a few weeks previously. Nonetheless, all these and other measures did not save his government.

On 8 May 1945 Travis, only a name to most people working in BP, sent a message to people working in the Park in which he combined thanks and warnings against giving anything away. It could not be published outside BP and on the day the war ended he was himself outside the Park in America:

> On this ever memorable day, I desire that all who are doing duty in this Organisation should be made aware of

my unbounded admiration for the way in which they have carried out their allotted tasks.

Such have been the difficulties, such has been the endeavour, and such have been the constant triumphs that one senses that words of gratitude from one individual are perhaps out of place. The personal knowledge of the contribution made towards winning the war is surely the real measure of the thanks which so rightly belong to one and all in a great and inspired organisation which I have the privilege to direct.

This is your finest hour.

The word 'day', not 'hour', stands out in my reading of this message from on high, as had Churchill's 'Action This Day'. As I explained in the first chapter of this book, I quite deliberately chose 'Secret Days' as the main title. Travis wrote of 8 May as 'this memorable day'. He was wrong, however, to use the adjective constant before the noun triumphs. No two days were alike for code-breakers. There were frustrating days as well as days of excitement, even of exhilaration. Nevertheless, I responded warmly to his sense of privilege. From below I regarded serving at BP as a very special privilege as much as he did from on high. I still do.

I like the long message sent out by teleprinter on 8 May 1945 by Squadron Leader Eric Jones 'to all out-stations':

Five long years we have waited for this day. We might all be waiting still if it were not for the folk who did a little more than wait – they worked and amongst those who worked no-one can claim to have worked harder or more effectively than the members of this section.

It has been a dreary heart-breaking job – always working against time on a manual task which needed brainwork as well. To find anyone who can combine both is not easy but all of you have shown that it could be done if the will to do it was there. There has been no glamour – no outward praise and even now you cannot return to your homes and tell them of your part in this war – and what a part it was.

This message was received by Jo Matthews at the Adstock out-station. The second half of it had a more personal touch:

I have nagged and ordered, instructed and moaned, and now I would like to apologise to you all for this pestering and I want to thank you all from the bottom of my heart for backing me up through thick and thin. This co-operation and the will to see a job through has rewarded us with the fact that we can claim more than most to have brought it – the day of days – forward to today

The title of my book echoes Jones's phrase 'day of days'. He ended his message realistically but reassuringly:

Again I thank you and now all being well we can take things easier until one by one we return eventually to civvies for good. It will be a sad day for many – and I specially will miss the honour of being head of the best section of ladies and gentlemen anyone could wish to have.

I still pause, however, when I examine and re-examine the implications of the adjective 'secret' in the title of this book. Travis, and Menzies above him, insisted in 1945 that we should all remain as secret in peacetime about what we had been doing at BP as we had in wartime. They never put the question for how long? There were certainly reasons for keeping all our secrets until we got home, but could we not then say something? For example, could we not have been allowed to say that we had been involved in secret intelligence? I did say that myself. After all I had been in the Intelligence Corps!

Before I got back home I had already begun to ponder in whatever time that I had in BP on the strengths and limitations of cryptographic intelligence. Subsequently, years later, I found two wartime assessments of its role that were very much to the point. The first, buried away in the Public Record Office, were memoranda from Rear-Admiral John Godfrey, Director of Naval Intelligence from 1939 to 1943, the man whom Churchill preferred to Menzies in 1939 for the post of 'C' after Sinclair's death. 'Intelligence', Godfrey wrote in a memorandum of 1941, 'is only rarely dramatic; its true basis is research, and the best results are usually obtained from the continuous study of insignificant details which, though singly of little value, are collectively of great importance.'

I knew the truth of that judgement by the time I left BP in 1945, but I did not then appreciate how dramatic a contrast to our own approach was evident in much of Godfrey's wartime intelligence work. He loved drama, and it was characteristic of him that within the Admiralty he selected as his personal assistant Ian Fleming, designated as NID 17F, who after the war modelled his 'M' on Godfrey. Together the two men planned daring and dangerous operations, one of them called Goldeneye, 'keeping an eye on Franco's Spain'. Goldeneye was the name which Fleming chose after the war for his Jamaican house where he wrote his James Bond novels. The women in them were somewhat different from the hundreds of women who worked in BP.

Fleming, as part of his wartime duties, visited BP regularly. It was because of stringent security rules that he could not mention BP in any of his novels. No one was more impressed by the need for such rules than Godfrey, but he was prepared to overlook all rules in responding to an early Fleming proposal in September 1940 to crash in the Channel a captured German bomber, flown by a British pilot wearing German uniform and speaking fluent German. He would send out an SOS signal in plain language and be picked up by a German rescue boat, whose crew would be shot.

Valuable information would then be brought back to England, information which would enable BP to break the naval Enigma cypher. Godfrey secured a plane and chose a pilot to carry out Operation Ruthless, but for various reasons – to the annoyance of Turing – it never took place. There were Bond-like cadences in Fleming's language – 'obtaining the loot', 'all blood and bandages'. This was not quite the style of Godfrey's own language. He also framed the cool precept: 'The value of a source [an intelligence source] is almost invariably greater than any given piece of information that source produces.' Putting that precept into practice meant protecting terms like 'Special', 'Ultra' and 'Top Ultra'. It also meant restricting the distribution of documents bearing these privileged words.

The second of my sources for meditation on intelligence was Brigadier E. T. Williams, whom I mentioned briefly in my first chapter. He deserves a full biography. He had joined up in 1939 as a 2nd lieutenant in the King's Dragoon Guards, but rose rapidly as a staff officer in the Eighth Army in North Africa. As chief intelligence officer to Montgomery he supplied his commander with Ultra information, which gave Monty the assurance to win the confidence of his men, most of whom had never heard of 'intelligence' let alone Ultra. He stayed at Monty's side and was with him in France in the 21st Army Group after the Allied landings on D-Day, taking care to visit BP before the landings to find out what intelligence BP could and would provide. He also wanted to give a picture of how events might develop after the Allied return to continental Europe. I did not hear him then or meet him, but I got to know him well as a friend and colleague after we were both made fellows of Oxford colleges.

In a note dated 5 October 1945 on the 'use of ultra', itself marked Top Secret Ultra, he gave the most detailed account of its use in the field that I have ever read, in the process comparing it with other sources of intelligence like Y analysis, air photography and agents' reports. 'It was forbidden to discuss Ultra on the telephone overseas. This rule was daily and hourly disobeyed . . . We broke the rules because they were unworkable.' Like most rules concerning security, they had been drawn up 'without consultation with the consumer', and he had to interpret them in his own way. He began his note with the reactions of consumers.

Ultra material was 'dangerously valuable' not only because consumers 'might lose it' but also because it seemed the answer to an intelligence officer's prayer, and by providing this answer it was liable to discourage the recipient from acquiring other kinds of intelligence. 'Instead of being the best, it tended to become the only source.' Moreover, despite the 'amazing speed' with which Ultra messages were received, it was, of course, usually out of date. The fact that it was more up-to-date than almost any other source tended to make those who read it forget this 'time lag'. At an army HQ 'we maintained that we had not done our day's work properly' unless Ultra information had been incorporated in 'our thinking'. Williams drew a distinction between an army HQ and an army group HQ. At an army HQ the interest was tactical, 'in battle stuff'. At an army group intelligence officers tried 'to beat the big strategic drum'.

Williams framed his own precepts. At whatever level of command, the duty of the intelligence staff was to explain what the enemy was doing and not to suggest how to defeat him. The African campaign in which he had taken part was, he suggested, 'but a frontier incident which enabled us to train an Army'.

I was sure of the necessity of precepts and rules behind the scenes in BP during the last months of the war when there was a decrease in the total number of Enigma messages which we were trying to break and when the enemy presented us with specific cryptographic problems of a technical kind. In intelligence terms that meant that we could not keep up to date the intelligence that we were supplying. In cryptographic terms it meant that non-mathematicians in the Watch had to leave the problems in the hands of mathematicians. Knowledge of message content that would be of interest to intelligence was irrelevant: content was relevant only if studying repeats could add to the mathematicians' understanding and give them the opportunity for a breakthrough.

Hut Eight faced even bigger difficulties in dealing with naval traffic. Since November 1944 the Germans had introduced individual keys for each operational U-Boat, and these were almost impossible to break. Then, on 1 February 1945, the Luftwaffe too implemented a decision which had been long expected in BP. Call-sign encryptions were to be changed daily and frequencies every three days. This was the worst blow that the Watch ever suffered, but it would have been a bigger blow if the Germans had implemented the decision earlier, before the Ardennes offensive.

Again, however, the situation changed for the better after documents relating to the new system were captured in the middle of March, and with Army Enigma now concentrated on Puffin and Falcon there was a record number of Army decrypts. The last turn of BP's fortunes had little to do with cryptography. As Germany disintegrated there was a sharp fall in the volume of both Luftwaffe and Army traffic. In consequence the volume of decrypts fell too.

On 29 April Jones issued what I thought to be a sensible order to all staff in Hut Three restricting the circulation outside BP of decrypts of messages of a 'spectacular' type relating to the fate of well-known Nazi personalities and to the scale of German capitulations. The popular press, with no such restraints imposed on it, made the most of the spectacular element in the news. On 12 April President Roosevelt died, and eighteen days later Hitler committed suicide in his Berlin bunker, along with Eva Braun, his mistress. Joseph Goebbels and his wife followed them after murdering their six children. After twelve years the Thousand Year Reich was ending in ignominy.

Might there have been an alternative ending? Before his fifty-sixth birthday on 20 April there was talk, not least in Hut Six, of Hitler and his entourage moving to an Alpine redoubt south of Munich, and I confess that, until he made it clear to Nazi leaders that he would die in his Berlin bunker 50 feet below ground, I myself felt that there could well be a Wagnerian ending to the war in far-away Berchtesgaden. So apparently did the American General Omar Bradley, who had been led to believe that there would be a Nazi retreat to the mountains far away from Berlin. He had reasons for believing so. Cornelius Ryan, author of *The Last Battle*, discussed in his book a large map that was kept on the wall in Eisenhower's headquarters and was headed 'Unconfirmed Installation in Reported Redoubt Area'. It displayed a range of symbols indicating food, ammunition, petrol dumps and factories. Not surprisingly many people who looked at the map were sceptical.

According to the British official history *Victory in the West*, for Hitler himself the notion of a redoubt was 'no more than a momentary idea that passed through his mind only to vanish again immediately afterwards'. Fully aware of the difference between rumour and fact, and, as I have written earlier, always sceptical about official histories, I was irritated to note that this sweeping judgement was relegated to an appendix.

When I had finished writing this chapter I read a British memorandum drafted by a representative of the British Chiefs of Staff and sent to the Combined Chiefs of Staff (British and American) explaining that they were concerned about the possible leakage of information regarding special intelligence when Allied historians started to examine German archives and compare them with those in Britain and in America. Already as the war ended various German archives were being sorted and translated. A directive should be agreed upon, the British Chiefs of Staff suggested, telling official historical sections that they would not be given access to special intelligence material and that all official histories prepared for publication would have to be submitted to 'the relevant security authority to ensure that no unwitting compromise of source has occurred'.

After appointing an *ad hoc* committee to consider the British memorandum, the American Joint Chiefs of Staff broadly speaking concurred, but asked for further clarification, pointing to different military and naval terminologies in the two countries. The British memorandum had suggested that official histories should deal only with important battles, a serious limitation, and should be written by 'personnel already indoctrinated', a further fundamental limitation.

The Americans did not take up these points in detail, but they stated what the British had not stated, that it would be naïve not to admit that signals intelligence sources had produced valuable information. They maintained that the only criterion should be security, a word not used in the British memorandum. The disturbing word 'indoctrination' was used again by the British when they passed on a revised General Directive and Indoctrination Brief for the 'appropriate authorities' in Canada, Australia, New Zealand and the USA for 'consideration and concurrence'.

This was an ironical twist to events at the German war's ending.

## Chapter 8

# Getting Outside BP

An alternative title for this chapter, far more jazzy, would have been *Show Me the Way to Go Home*. That was the title of the fortnightly unjazzy Bulletin No. 78 of the Army Bureau of Current Affairs, dated 23 September 1944, several months before the final events described at the end of the last chapter. The subtitle of the Bulletin cast aside all jazz: it included the word 'official'. This, the bulletin explained, was 'the official PLAN OF RELEASE' from the forces, 'explained and illustrated'.

Written months before the war ended by Major General A. J. K. Pigott, Director of Recruiting and Demobilisation, the bulletin began by describing 'the present war as the most astonishing and unpredictable story ever written', not quite the way in which the Second World War is usually described in the twenty-first century. 'No composer of thrillers in film or fiction', Pigott explained, 'could excel such a sequence of captions' as the ones that he had selected, 'Two Million Frenchmen Surrender', 'London's Burning', 'Egypt in Peril', 'the Japs Sink an American Fleet', 'Will Moscow Fall?', 'A German Army Bites the Desert Dust', and 'The Modern Nero Gets the Knock-out'.

Pigott stressed that the war was not yet over. 'Premature jubilation is still imprudent. We have got much in the bag, but not all.' His phrasing was less eloquent than the German General von Arnim's Enigma signal to Berlin after German resistance in

Tunisia collapsed in May 1943, 'We have fired our last cartridge. We are closing down for ever.' There were ample surprises to come in BP in the months between May 1943 and 23 September 1944 and in the months between then and VE-Day, 8 May 1945. The war against Japan was still to be won. Derek Taunt, scrutinizing from inside BP what still seemed to him an uncertain present, recalled that VJ-Day, 15 August, followed VE-Day 'sooner than we had expected'. He noted more generally, in retrospect, that the nature of the Japanese defeat had shattered all precedents.

BP perspectives on the war, as I showed in my last chapter, were quite different from outside perspectives until the dropping of the atomic bomb drew insiders and outsiders together. Patrick Wilkinson wrote movingly that his last, lasting and chilling memory of BP was 'the evening when we were about to have supper in the cafeteria and someone came in and reported the dropping of the atomic bomb on Hiroshima. The news was received in dead silence.'

Many of us had left BP before these strange days when relief was mingled with horror. By the end of August total staff numbers were down from 8,900 to 5,500, and a month after VJ-Day Commander Travis declared that GC&CS was no longer operational. In the spring of 1946 the last person left inside BP, Barbara Abernethy, closed the premises down, locking the huts and the gates and taking the key down to 114 Lime Grove, Eastcote, the wartime bombe out-station about fifteen miles north-west of London. Barbara had come to BP at the age of eighteen in 1939, before war was declared. She married Joe Eachus, who, as a young US Navy lieutenant, had been one of the first two Americans to visit BP in March 1942 'to tell Washington what was happening in Bletchley Park'.

By the time that Barbara arrived at Eastcote, some of the people who had been working at BP were by then ensconced there in what was now the London Signals Intelligence Centre. Travis remained in charge of it until 1952, to be succeeded by Eric Jones who had put into order the troubled affairs of Hut Three and become its head in 1942. In 1948 the name London Signals Intelligence Centre was formally changed to GCHQ.

There was continuity in all this. For those who moved on into GCHQ a similar kind of work was being carried on in the new setting as in the old. There had been no real sense of an ending. Like BP, suburban Eastcote was a place of secrets, and the number of people employed inside it tripled to 3,000 between 1945 and 1948. Those who had moved there from BP had done so in four batches; the first of them included the Soviet and East European divisions. The last batch moved in April 1946. Some of my colleagues in the Hut Six Watch were among them. I never heard from any of them again. I have read subsequently that when newcomers to Eastcote were seeking lodgings they were not allowed to make any reference to signals intelligence. They could, however, say that they worked in GCHQ.

Long before the fourth batch left I had left BP – and intelligence – for the last time without ceremony and, as far as I can remember, without any word of thanks. I left the Camp in cheerful mood on 7 August 1945, carrying a railway pass to Bedford to join my Commandant, Colonel Fillingham – at his invitation – as RSM, this time a real RSM, of No. 5 Formation College at Howbury Hall, over which he was given command. Formation Colleges, I was told, were 'at the apex of the Army Education Scheme', but I did not know how their sites had been chosen. Ours was not far from Bedford, but it seemed remote and was not easy to get at. I was glad that my baggage, including a small library of books, was forwarded on afterwards. Subsequently, out of uniform, I got to know other Formation Colleges as well. Their purpose was to help troops prepare for their return to civilian life. Among them was the school set up by Scottish Command at Newbattle Abbey, Dalkeith, the only college housed in premises that had previously been used for adult education.

Howbury Hall was almost as unusual an institution as Shenley Road Camp when Fillingham commanded it. Captain E. Bickerstaffe, who as a lieutenant had been Fillingham's adjutant there, moved to Howbury Hall with him. Unlike BP, Howbury Hall was a place entirely without secrets. I could now tell my mother and father just what I was doing, and on learning what I was doing they were not in the least surprised. I made it abundantly clear to them, however, that it was not what I had been doing during the war. Fillingham and Bickerstaffe knew that without being told. In many ways my short spell with Fillingham at Howbury Hall, where we no longer thought in terms of days, had a bigger influence on the rest of my life than the 700 secret days that I spent at BP. At the time they briefly changed my way of life. For one thing I was genuinely in authority as a real RSM, upheld with Fillingham's support. I was in a land not of secrets but of standing orders. I would never be in that position again.

In the long run the Formation College gave me the chance of establishing, with Fillingham's blessing, a foothold both in broadcasting and in army education. From the time of joining the Army, egged on by my 'comrades', a word we would never have thought of using, I had frequently taken part in Army Bureau of Current Affairs discussions, which greatly varied in the interest they aroused and in the scale of participation. Now I was drawn into similar discussions all the time. In my view, then and since, the man who created ABCA, William Emrys Williams, born in 1896, was one of the compelling visionaries of his generation. Many strands were woven together in his own life. When still in his thirties he was secretary of the British Institute of Adult Education, a Welsh protégé of the behind-the-scenes *éminence grise*, Thomas Jones, secretary of the Pilgrim Trust – and much else – who had been Lloyd George's closest confidant.

Williams believed as an article of faith in the power of people to shape their own futures, and ABCA Bulletin 63, *This Business of Public Opinion*, explained how he saw this happening. He directed the Army Bureau of Current Affairs from 1941 to 1945, converting it after the war into the Bureau of Current Affairs. From 1936 to 1965 he was a director of Penguin Books whose products, for me as for many servicemen, were a source both of knowledge and of pleasure, and during the war he also played an important part in the organization of CEMA, the Council for the Encouragement of Music and the Arts, founded in 1940, which under the chairmanship of John Maynard Keynes became the Arts Council.

Two of the last series of ABCA bulletins before *Show Me the Way to Go Home* were entitled *Work for All* (No. 71) and *Schools for Tomorrow* (No. 76). In the five years after leaving the Army in September 1945 I gave many lectures on the subjects I had worked on in the Formation College to troops scattered throughout the world. I had made my debut with the BBC as a Forces Educational Service broadcaster writing scripts while still in uniform, and presenting them on the Forces Programme. In my post-war talks to troops in Gibraltar and Berlin in 1946 and 1947 I left both BP – and Oxford – far behind me, emphasizing, as did Pigott, who had never had anything to do with BP, that the war had global and not local and national dimensions, and that its outcome was 'determined as much in the factory and the coal-pit as in the battle zones'. I never mentioned intelligence, let alone BP.

Hugh Alexander, chess champion. Alexander became the head cryptanalyst in Hut Eight. He was one of the signatories of the famous letter to Churchill in 1941.

Harry Hinsley, the brilliant boy from Walsall, who won the trust of Naval Intelligence at BP and after the war wrote BP's official history.

Bletchley station. Its main social amenity for BPites was the Coffee Tavern, situated behind where the ladies are standing.

Assembling electrical equipment at BTM's Letchworth factory, where BP's bombes were made. In peacetime many of these women worked in the Spirella corset factory.

Women at work in the Machine Room of Hut Six in the summer of 1943. Here the good news came through by telephone that the bombes had broken an Enigma key.

Conveying messages in Hut Six, Block D. A system perhaps derived from retailing and the John Lewis connection of several prominent BPites?

The Decoding Room in Hut Six. The women are using modified Typex machines to simulate Enigmas.

A Tunny machine of the Fish family. The great Colossus was devised to read Tunny messages.

This machine may not look too reminiscent of the work of the cartoonist Heath Robinson, but that is why it got its name. The first Robinson arrived in BP in May 1943, before Colossus, and needed many people to work it.

Colossus (*above & below*) needed careful attention. The Wrens handling it were diligently supervised by, among others, Shaun Wylie. The Wrens thought him 'absolutely wonderful'. He married one of them.

*Left:* Three American friends outside their camp at Little Brickhill. On the left is Frank Stanton, song writer, who had nothing to do with Frank Stanton, radio entrepreneur. I took this photograph. I wish that I had taken more.

*Below:* Inside BP with American friends. Like them I wore a tie.

*Below right:* The cover of the programme of one of BP's intimate revues, appropriately titled.

*Bottom, right:* Invitation to an American dance from Telford Taylor.

Some of the staff of Hut Six pose for a celebration photograph on VE-Day. Howard Smith is the last standing person fully visible on the right, with his wife kneeling in front of him. John Manisty is the very last on the right. I was celebrating outside BP.

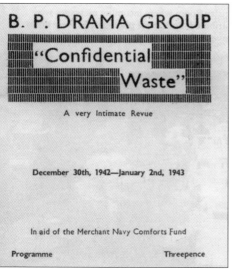

# B. P. DRAMA GROUP

## "Confidential Waste"

A very Intimate Revue

December 30th, 1942—January 2nd, 1943

In aid of the Merchant Navy Comforts Fund

Programme                    Threepence

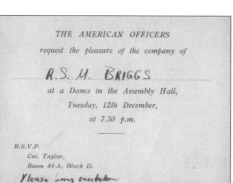

*THE AMERICAN OFFICERS*

*request the pleasure of the company of*

R.S. M. Briggs

*at a Dance in the Assembly Hall,*

*Tuesday, 12th December,*

*at 7.30 p.m.*

R.S.V.P.
Col. Taylor,
Room 44-A, Block D.
Please bring invitation

---

CORN EXCHANGE, BEDFORD
Wednesday, 10 February 1943 at 7.15 p.m.

# BBC SYMPHONY CONCERT

| | |
|---|---|
| Overture, Beatrice and Benedict | BERLIOZ (1803-1869) |
| Concerto in D for Violin and Orchestra (Op. 35) | TCHAIKOVSKY (1840-1893) |

*INTERVAL*

| | |
|---|---|
| Symphony | WILLIAM WALTON Born 1902 |

*Solo Violin:*
HENRY HOLST

THE BBC SYMPHONY ORCHESTRA
Leader: Paul Beard

Conductor: CLARENCE RAYBOULD

*Programme Price*
*Sixpence*

The BBC Symphony Orchestra was evacuated to Bedford during the war and stayed there until 1946. It became a great local attraction, with BPites as a main part of the audience.

With a group of colleagues from Hut Six, photographed near the BP lake in 1945 in a mix of uniforms and civilian clothes. The photograph pays no more attention to rank than our working lives did. Ione Jay is kneeling on the extreme left.

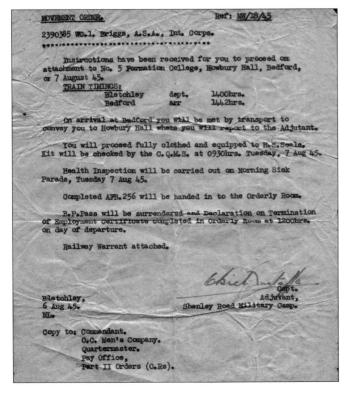

My exit from BP. The movement order for my transfer to No. 5 Formation College. It was on the other side of Bedford.

Nevertheless, in my post-war talks to troops I was conscious of one personal link with BP. In the book that I wrote there, *Patterns of Peacemaking*, I had taken up some of the themes of ABCA bulletins such as *Are We United Nations?* (No. 55), *Relief, European Friends in Need* (No. 74) and *Armies of Occupation* (No. 60). My approach in my book, 'learning from last time', was the same as Pigott's, if less didactic in the language that I used, and it was the fact that I had written it and that it was in the press which persuaded Worcester College to give me a fellowship.

This guaranteed that I would get an early Class B Release from the Army before the Oxford Michaelmas Term began in October 1945. I felt as much trepidation about the prospect as I had done when I entered Hut Six. For several months before I got my release I had been given a room in the college, a very old room, not too clean and somewhat dilapidated, which seemed very different from my hut room in the Camp.

In many ways the Formation College was more like a university than BP had been. It was there that I discussed most of the academic work that had been pushed aside after I left Cambridge, meeting and arguing with future academics, particularly Captain Sammy Finer, a graduate of Oxford, who had served in the Royal Signals Corps, mainly in the Middle East. He was a vociferous talker who shared, indeed extended, my interest in such subjects as public health and, a curious combination, science fiction. I already preferred reading novels about the future to reading novels about the past. I was also getting interested in sociology, not then a much-studied subject. Finer was to be one of the first professors appointed to Keele University College in North Staffordshire by the Master of Balliol, A. D. (later Lord) Lindsay, and I was Keele's first external examiner. Keele was the inspiration of Lindsay, who had clear ideas of what a university college should be.

Before I moved to the Formation College, I had decided while still at BP to attend a course on business studies at the City of London College, from 8 to 12 July 1945, and it was there that I had my first encounter in the classroom with management issues. More immediately to the point it was in Marylebone Road of all places that I first found myself treated as a real RSM, marching soldiers from a hotel used by the military to Baker Street underground station and late in the day marching them back again – I felt more like the 'Grand old Duke of York' than I was to do with Fillingham. Despite this responsibility I passed the course with distinction and met other soldier students on it, all under the auspices of Eastern Command, with whom I stayed in touch after the war as I did with Finer.

Stanley Bishop, a sergeant in the Royal Tank Corps, was a good person to engage with: I admired the way in which he combined an interest in music with an interest in business. I was best man at his wedding in Frome, and godfather to his son. I was at the stage of my life where I was establishing new personal relationships and discovering new places.

The news of my Class B Release from Howbury Hall reached me not by post nor from the adjutant. Late one night, after 11 p.m., which night I cannot recall, I was summoned to Colonel Fillingham's office. He told me that he had just received 'bad news' – my Class B release had come – and he asked me to sit down and talk it over. 'You will be leaving at a difficult time, but I hope that you will continue to help me until you start term in Oxford.' And then he added, totally unconventionally, 'While we are talking there are three things that I feel I must tell you. First, keep a diary. Second, beware the insidious [or was it invidious?] influence of women. Third, when you get to Oxford try to get me an honorary degree: I would like to wear a gown over my uniform.'

Clearly the importance of these three pieces of what he thought of as advice were in inverse order. The first clearly was guidance that I liked: I would like to have kept a diary, as many generals did, during the war. The second was, I felt, meant entirely for me, although might also have been related to Fillingham's personal experience. The third was a request that I knew I could not meet. I did not then know what an honorary degree was, but I knew that when I got to Oxford I would be in no position to get Fillingham one. I did promise, however, that I would continue to help him to the best of my ability until I got to Oxford. We then shook hands, I stood to attention and saluted, and left his office.

I will deal with what happened to me when I got back to Oxford in my next chapter. After I left the Army I stayed for a weekend with one of the fellows of the college in his beautifully furnished eighteenth-century house near the Forest of Dean, after I had travelled from Bedford to Northampton to collect the civilian clothes which demobilized members of the forces received when they cast their uniforms aside. I managed to get a non-Sunday-best type of suit which fitted me, and a hat which I immediately discarded. One of the delights of leaving the Army was never to have to wear a forage cap again.

For those in the Intelligence Corps who stayed at BP after VE-Day 'getting out' could be a far from straightforward matter. As they became redundant, wherever they were going next, they often had to make their way, not necessarily immediately, to the Intelligence Corps depot at Wentworth Woodhouse. Doubtless it was a more agreeable experience for them than it had been for me when I had travelled to Rotherham in the great move north from King Alfred's College, Winchester, in 1942 and I was glad I never had to go back there after the summer of 1943. I can understand the elation felt by Eric Plant when he, among a group of sixteen

BPites, arrived in Rotherham from Bedford in October 1945. 'The North, the North', he cried. But very soon he and fifteen others left the north and moved out to Germany where they joined the Army of Occupation. One of the party was Jimmy Thirsk, who then spent several months in Field Security checking barge traffic on the Rhine and was not demobilized until March 1946. There were many other duties for Intelligence Corps officers and non-commissioned officers in Germany, such as rounding up war criminals, and one prominent officer at BP, Captain Jerry Roberts, a German linguist who had worked in the Testery, spent two years in Germany after the war attached to the War Crimes Investigation Unit before being demobilized. He found his post-war work far less interesting than his time in the Testery.

Without a Class B Release it was difficult for a serviceman to get out of uniform even if he had no job to perform. The demobilization scheme, promulgated in September 1944 by Ernest Bevin, Minister of Labour and from 1945 Foreign Secretary, applied both to men and women. They were to be released according to their age and service number, the latter registering the length of their service. Married women, and men aged 50 or more, were given immediate priority, but there were relatively few of these in BP which seemed a forlorn place long before Barbara Abernethy locked the gates.

Civilian workers at BP fared worse even than men and women in uniform; some of them were told bluntly and not necessarily face-to-face that they were now redundant. They were not to receive any recognition until the first decade of the twenty-first century. The fact that in 1945 they were not allowed, in my view unfairly, to say anything of what they had been doing in BP and that they were given no record of their work or rank was a very serious handicap. The ones who went back to their old jobs were the luckiest, but they did not always find it easy to 'fit in'. Welchman, who could have gone back to Sidney Sussex, recalled in the 1970s that he had been 'thoroughly shaken' out of his old academic life by his 'challenging experiences'. When he got out of BP he took up, as I noted earlier, his colleague Hugh Alexander's old post at the John Lewis Partnership.

No adequate record remains of what happened to most of the people who worked in BP, either civilians or men and women in uniform. We still lack any overall vista. The Americans went home quickly, and some of them continued their education under the GI Bill of Rights. There was no such Bill in Britain.

## Chapter 9

# Oxford

Three critical days in my life had all started soon after D-Day in 1944 after I came off night shift on 12 July. I went over to Cambridge on the 13th and saw Herbert Butterfield at his house. He offered me a research fellowship at Peterhouse, 'a very good offer' I wrote in my diary 'with many tempting sides'. The next day, a Friday, I went to Worcester College, Oxford, where I found the Dean, C. H. Wilkinson, who also commanded the Officers' Training Corps, 'forbidding and irritating', and the historian, H. V. F. Somerset, who knew something about BP and had visited the camp, 'hospitable and convivial'. Before leaving Oxford on Saturday 15th and returning via Buckingham to my night shift at BP, I met the Provost, then aged eighty-three, and the Vice-Provost, then aged seventy-nine. Both of them talked at length on their having suffered the privations of war.

All went well with me, for on 8 August, before the formalities of a College meeting, Somerset wrote to me in an up-beat letter that I had been invited to a fellowship and tutorship in politics and economics at Worcester. 'Great news putting me in high spirits,' I wrote in my diary. 'At last a career assured.' Butterfield, whom I informed at once, replied that he could not compete with Worcester's offer. I was not surprised. As much of a canny Yorkshireman as Butterfield himself was, I had already decided that I should accept a full fellowship and tutorship in Oxford

144

rather than a research fellowship in Cambridge. I told Harold Laski, who understood at once, that I would not be taking up my Gerstenberg Studentship at the LSE.

There was, nevertheless, a further choice to be made, which I did not mention to Somerset, Butterfield or, indeed, to Laski, who as Chairman of the Labour Party would doubtless have wanted to give me his own advice on how I should make it. On 11 August I received an invitation from Elland Labour Party in Yorkshire, to contest the seat there, which I knew to be winnable. This put me in a quandary, for not only my local Labour MP since 1942, Ivor Thomas, who had taken up the seat on the death of the previous Labour MP, but also, high up in the Party, Hugh Dalton wanted me to go into politics. Dalton, whom I had met twice during the war, was looking for suitable candidates from the forces and felt that I was particularly promising as a Cambridge graduate in uniform – and a warrant officer at that. Ivor Thomas and I had both been stewards at Roy Jenkins's wedding in the Savoy Chapel earlier in 1944, and it was there that I met Attlee for the first time.

Roy, who had finished his degree, was already looking for a constituency, first pinning his hopes on Aston in Birmingham where he was drawn into a contest for the nomination with, among others, Woodrow Wyatt, who won it. Politics beckoned them in a way that it never beckoned me. Roy, the son of a Welsh Labour MP, was disappointed but not deterred when he failed to win the nomination, whereas I, a 23-year-old who knew little about either academic or political ways of life, disliked being forced to choose between an academic and a political career.

Fortunately, as I can see in retrospect, I chose right. I would have found it difficult to accept the discipline of a political party. More important, there were particular academic projects that positively attracted me, one of them coincidentally, given Roy's continuing search for a Birmingham seat, an historical study of Joseph Chamberlain and Birmingham politics. Roy, who was to write about Balfour, Gladstone and Churchill, never showed any interest in Chamberlain. I did not anticipate that he would become a greatly admired historian.

I received other invitations to stand for constituencies that I did not know later in 1944; several of them were winnable and were indeed won in the general election the next year. They did not tempt me. Nevertheless, I widened my experience of politics in that election, helping Roy to fight the unwinnable seat of Solihull. I drove around its to me unknown streets in an open car (and in battledress), telling all who could hear me that they ought to make the most of the opportunity of voting in the first general election for ten years. I also gave one of the longest and most difficult speeches of my life to a packed hall of Roy's enthusiastic supporters anxiously waiting for their candidate to appear on the eve of the poll. Neither of us, of course, could refer to Bletchley in what we said, but the word intelligence was mentioned.

I met quite a different circle of voters when I stayed with Somerset just after the Labour victory. The first of them was a woman of great wealth from a family of northern industrialists turned into west country gentry. 'They'll soon find out that they can't do without us,' she murmured to me as we strolled through her rose garden. After that to me shocking remark I could not hide my views from Somerset who, while not sharing my sense of shock, saw the absurdity of such a comment. I did not try to hide my views either from the Chaplain and Bursar of Worcester College, R. L. P. Milburn, whose political stance was also quite different from mine.

As a graduate of Sidney Sussex College, Cambridge, Milburn linked the two colleges, one in Cambridge, one in Oxford, with which I was now linking myself. He knew the importance of my work at BP and he welcomed to his house more than one girl whom I had met in BP. He was an amusing raconteur and had a fascinating career of his own which took him from Worcester College to the deanship of Worcester Cathedral and from there to the chapel of the Inner Temple. He became a very good friend. He also kept an impressive diary. I had never met such a keen diarist before.

My first aged provost, C. J. Lys, about whom Milburn loved to tell stories, did not keep a diary, but he liked talking to a young man he had only just met about his own early life. There was a coincidence there too. Lys had been educated at Sherborne as Turing, failing Marlborough, had been. Lys could never have heard of Turing, but he may have known about the Turing family.

The next provost of Worcester, J. C. Masterman, would quite likely have heard of Turing and would not have been surprised that years later memorials would be put up to him. I myself spent six months at the Institute of Advanced Studies in 1953, and I did talk about him a little then to some of the brilliant young physicists I met there. When Masterman made it clear that he was interested in the headship of Worcester College, I was far and away the youngest member of a small delegation of fellows of the college who walked to Christ Church to invite Masterman to become provost. His friend Cyril Wilkinson, the Dean of Worcester, who knew Masterman well, was the senior member of the delegation.

My special pleasure at his election was his connection with intelligence. I worked with him closely for eight years and for the whole of that time he was the only person in Worcester College, and, indeed, the only head of any Oxford college, with whom I could discuss matters of intelligence. I did so rarely, but when the

Korean War broke out Masterman called me into the provost's lodgings and asked me whether I would like to go back into intelligence again. He was disappointed when I said no. In 1952 Leonard Palmer had been appointed Professor of Comparative Philology in Oxford, and a fellow of the college and, since he had been in Hut Four at BP when I first met him, I was able to tell him about the question that Masterman had put to me. He was amused, but not surprised.

Masterman was a born kingmaker, and when I became provost myself in 1976 – with Oliver Franks in between – to greet my return to Worcester he presented me with a copy of his book *The Double-Cross System in the War of 1939 to 1945*, published in 1972. He had uncontentiously written this book, which he called a secret 'report', between July and September 1945 while I was in Fillingham's Formation College, one of the few varieties of educational institution about which Masterman knew nothing.

There was no shortage of contention, however, behind the scenes, at various points between 1945 and 1972, when his book was published by Yale University Press in America and Oxford University Press in Britain, two years before Winterbotham's revelations. Throughout the contentions Masterman had been supported in the long struggle to get his book published by his close friend, the Earl of Swinton, a Conservative politician, very knowledgeable about intelligence, who among many other official duties had been Chairman of the Security Executive from 1940 to 1942.

During the First World War Masterman had been interned in Germany, where he was studying when war broke out, and during the Second World War he had gone into intelligence, quickly becoming a junior officer in MI5, and going on to play a key role in the evolution of the double-cross system of organised deception. As he grew old he became more and more determined to get his internally commissioned 'secret report' published for what he hoped would be a large readership, mainly on the ground that, in circumstances very different from those of 1945, it would be of value to MI5 if his report was converted into a book.

With many old pupils in high places, some of them in intelligence, Masterman seemed to be in a very strong position to get his own way. The three most important of them were Dick White, born in 1910, who was in turn head of MI5 and MI6, a unique double; Denis Greenhill, a senior diplomat raised to a baronetcy, whose last job was as Permanent Under-Secretary of State at the Foreign Office; and Alec Douglas-Home, for a brief period Prime Minister before Harold Wilson, and later Foreign Secretary under Edward Heath. Unfortunately for J. C. the first two were uneasy about the idea of *The Double-Cross System* being published and sold. Home was eventually to back him decisively, but Masterman was irritated when, having offered to cut out any offending passages and have his book published by the Oxford University Press, it made no difference. It was this rebuff that led him to pursue what he called his 'Plan Diabolo': to have the book published across the Atlantic by Yale University Press, which would require no omissions.

I got to know Dick White quite well during the 1960s, and discussed with him more than once (in secret) the whole issue of secrecy, but I never met Roger Hollis, an old Worcester man, who, as head of MI5 after White, was forced to deal not only with security scandals, the worst of them the Philby affair, but with scandalous stories about himself. One of these was that he had been a double agent.

The return of the Conservatives to power under Heath, a good Balliol man, in 1970 made no difference to Masterman's chances.

Politicians and senior civil servants not personally known to Masterman continued to withhold permission to publish, and in 1971 Peter Rawlinson, Heath's Attorney-General, expressed the opinion that if Masterman were to do so he would be committing an offence under the Official Secrets Act, with consequences that would be serious for him and the country.

There was much further coming and going behind the scenes with Rawlinson eventually deciding, doubtless after talks with Alec Douglas-Home, then Foreign Secretary, that if the book were published at all, it should be published simultaneously in the United States and in Britain. Douglas-Home strongly supported Masterman at this critical point. He had always respected his old tutor and now he is said to have asked his Cabinet colleagues, 'If I can't trust my old tutor, whom else can I trust?' Tutorial relationships remain strong. When Masterman died in 1988 I telephoned Douglas-Home, whom I did not know well, to invite him to deliver the memorial address at a service in honour of Masterman in Oxford Cathedral, situated in Christ Church, the right place for J. C. At once, over the phone, and without consulting a diary, he said yes.

Rawlinson's decision, rather more than a compromise, horrified the then head of MI5, Martin Furnival-Jones. Before the Attorney-General announced it Furnival-Jones had written angrily to Masterman that he considered that his determination to go ahead with publication was disgraceful:

> When you left the division after the war you signed an undertaking not to do precisely what you are proposing to do. So far as I am aware, this is the first time in more than sixty years of the history of the service that a former member has threatened to break his word in this way.

Masterman was not deterred by such an attack on him. Although he had ceased to be provost of Worcester in 1961, he was still living near the college in a college house when I became provost in 1976. I then spent some time – but not too much – going over the ground with him.

His was not a unique experience. There were other secret reports which were not to be published until long after Winterbotham. At BP all sections had been required to write up their wartime histories under the direction of Frank Birch (in charge of naval cryptography throughout the war). A secretary spent 1945 typing them. There were also individual reports, none of which were subsequently published. As a humble code-breaker I had myself written an essay in 1945 on what I thought would happen to cryptography after the war. I have never subsequently been able to see a copy of it, though I have often tried. The Cabinet Office has always been in the way. I recall that I used the word electronics.

I did not know Masterman's story in all its detail until 1972, but talking to him had kept me in touch not only with his affairs but with intelligence generally, and I was quietly and secretly consulted on various matters at more than one point in the story. In the late 1970s I also discussed the issue of security, which remains a difficult one, with Burke Trend, formerly head of the Cabinet Office, who had become a colleague of mine in Oxford as rector of Lincoln College in 1978. As head of the Cabinet Office he had believed, as I did, that in principle secrets should be kept. The idea of transparency, now very widely held, was slow to take hold, yet I objected even then in the 1970s, when many BP secrets were being divulged, to what I thought was a governmental obsession with secrecy.

I talked about this and the associated argument about security to the journalist Chapman Pincher, who had publicized the story of Philby's treachery. I liked Pincher, although he continued to voice his conviction that Hollis was a traitor in his best-selling book of 1981, *Their Trade is Treachery*. At the least what Pincher wrote forced the government to explain more clearly in Parliament just what role the intelligence services played. It was not until the 1990s that significant changes were made in procedures, and by then I was no longer provost of Worcester. I reached my retiring age of seventy in 1991.

The Oxford and Christ Church historian Hugh Trevor-Roper, born in 1914, was a pupil and friend of Masterman, who backed him loyally throughout his academic career which took him finally from Oxford to the mastership of Peterhouse, Cambridge, coincidentally (a real coincidence) the college in which I might have been a research fellow in 1945. Having published his best-selling book *The Last Days of Hitler* in 1947, which named Dick White as the person who had helped him most, Trevor-Roper, later Lord Dacre, was deeply involved in intelligence issues, far more than I was, for the rest of his life. Like Masterman after him, he discovered that behind the scenes there were powerful people, in this case Stewart Menzies, who objected to the publication of *Last Days*, but they were on less strong ground than the powerful people who objected later to Masterman's book. After all, *The Last Days of Hitler* was a genuinely new work. Trevor-Roper wrote it by hand in an exercise book; there was no official imprimatur.

During the war Trevor-Roper had served in intelligence, rising to the rank of major, and for a time he had broken coded Abwehr messages, though not those encrypted using Enigma machines. He knew from the inside how the double-agent system operated and, indeed, how important deception had been at many points during the war. But he had his own angle on BP. His relations with it had never been straightforward. His war service had begun with the RSS, the Radio Security Service, which was part not of the MI6 complex but of the War Office, and not MI5 as often thought.

In 1939 the RSS had moved its London base to Wormwood Scrubs, an ancient prison in a setting as different from Christ Church as any that could possibly be imagined. Like MI6, however, RSS depended on a jumble of places outside London. It was concerned with the interception and use of foreign radio messages collected from Army, Post Office and civilian operators who scanned short-wave frequencies looking for enemy wireless traffic that would assist MI5 to round up German spies.

This quest was somewhat unreal, for, as Trevor-Roper himself soon realised, the only two German spies operating in Britain when war broke out in 1939 had been detected by MI5 itself and turned into double agents, trusted both in Germany and in Britain. Arthur Owens, code-named 'Snow', gradually mustered a group of agents controlled from London by Colonel Tommy ('Tar') Robertson at MI5, head of a new section called B1a. Throughout the war he was in a position to run the whole German spy system concerned with Britain. This was the supreme example of deception. There were fifteen double agents operating at the time of the Normandy landings in June 1944, encouraging the Germans to believe that the Normandy landings were a feint attack and that the main Allied thrust would be against the Pas de Calais.

Each week the so-called Twenty Club met in the MI5 head-quarters in London to decide what true and what false and what misleading information to feed them with. Twenty was another way of expressing the roman numeral XX – or Double-Cross. Neither Hut Six nor Hut Three had anything to do with this process. Masterman chaired the weekly meetings of the Twenty Club, and after the war must have been impressed when one of his wartime colleagues, Ewan Montagu, published a book about a highly successful example of British deception techniques, *The Man Who Never Was*, in 1953, nearly twenty years before Masterman's *The Double Cross System* appeared.

In his own published book Masterman was not allowed to mention BP and its links with the breaking of Abwehr traffic, which in consequence leaves out a vital element in Britain's wartime deception strategy. Trevor-Roper had fewer qualms about briefly mentioning BP's work in reviews. At the time he knew of the visit that Denniston as head of GC&CS had paid to Wormwood Scrubs in 1940, accompanied by Oliver Strachey, to ensure that no cryptographic work would be carried on outside BP. Trevor-Roper suggested that BP should set up a special section to handle the Abwehr traffic some of which RSS had been breaking. In consequence, soon afterwards, he paid the first of his own visits to BP.

Over time he became a more and more difficult visitor, and eventually in 1942 he was rebuked from on high by Menzies for 'telling tales out of school' about MI6 to Desmond Morton, then Churchill's personal assistant, and Frederick Lindemann, recently made Lord Cherwell, Churchill's main scientific adviser. Travis denied Trevor-Roper all access to Huts Three and Four. By then, the positioning of RSS as an intelligence agency had completely changed following the report of a secret committee headed by Swinton which recommended in May 1941 that RSS should cease to be a part of the War Office and become part of SIS's Radio Communications section. Its new head, therefore, would be Richard Gambier-Parry (ex-BBC and radio manufacturing), who had run Station X when GC&CS moved to Bletchley. By 1941 he was a colonel, who chose as his operational 'controller', a BBC term, his friend Ted Maltby.

Trevor-Roper liked Gambier-Parry for the same reasons as Welchman liked Faulkner. He was a keen horseman and huntsman, and Trevor-Roper took an enthusiastic part in the Whaddon Hunt not far from Bletchley to which Leon had belonged and that Gambier-Parry presided over. He could not stand Maltby, however, whom he looked down upon as an obscure, ignorant business upstart. Nevertheless, in 'telling tales out of school' in 1942 about the failings of British intelligence he irritated Gambier-Parry as much as Maltby or Travis. His unrestrained language did not help. His superiors in SIS, he complained in an unpublished note, were 'a nest of timid and corrupt incompetents, concerned only with the security of their own discreditable existence'.

From within the confines of BP Nigel de Grey was provoked to ask Travis why, if Trevor-Roper's own master (Gambier-Parry) did not seem able to control him, how could 'we confide our secrets to him?' Meanwhile Trevor-Roper's Oxford friends warned him of the mischief that he was causing, not least for himself, by his oral outbursts and his behaviour. Thus, for instance, Sir Thomas Armstrong, organist at Christ Church and future principal (1955–68) of the Royal Academy of Music in London, told him that he was being 'false to his own intellectual nature' in going fox hunting and being such a snob.

This was criticism to which, for once, Trevor-Roper listened. Armstrong was a good friend, and when he left Oxford for London he handed over to Trevor-Roper, who had recently married Xandra, a daughter of Earl Haig, the tenancy of 8 St Aldate's, an early nineteenth-century house belonging to Christ Church. After he was appointed Regius Professor of History in 1957 Trevor-Roper had been required to leave Christ Church for Oriel. In 1979 he was made a peer and took the title Lord Dacre.

There are many twists and turns to the subsequent story. Armstrong's son, Robert, was to be one of Burke Trend's successors as head of the Cabinet Office, and in that capacity he had to deal with a book, *Spycatcher* (1987), written by a former MI5 officer, Peter Wright. The Thatcher government tried unsuccessfully to block the sale of the book anywhere in the world, and the Prime Minister ordered Armstrong to go to Australia to give evidence when Wright sought to prevent this. It was a hopeless journey and Wright won in the Australian court. Trevor-Roper no more liked then what he thought of as the government's obsession with secrecy than he had done during the war.

If only because of the wartime roles of Masterman and Trevor-Roper, Christ Church is the Oxford College to concentrate upon in writing about BP, as King's College is in writing about Cambridge and BP. It was in Christ Church too that M. R. D. Foot, who graduated from New College, was working on the Gladstone diaries when I settled in post-war Oxford. I used to talk to him more in the Savile Club in London than in Oxford, and I met there with him old members of SOE, which to begin with had been associated with Hugh Dalton, then the Minister of Economic Warfare and, in 1945, Chancellor of the Exchequer. Among many works dealing with resistance activities and special operations, Foot published an outline history of SOE in 1984 and in 2008 *Memoirs of an SOE Historian*. I became interested through him in the comparative history of SOE and BP.

Other Oxford colleagues of mine had been involved in BP, however, among them Leonard Palmer at Worcester, whom I have mentioned, the medieval historian John Prestwich, a fellow of Queen's, who had worked with him, and Frank Lepper, historian of the classical world and fellow of Corpus Christi College, where Lady Dacre's son by a previous marriage was also a fellow.

It is interesting to note how Oxford (and indeed Cambridge) dons described their BP days in their entries in *Who's Who*: the entries usually read simply 'Foreign Office', sometimes with the words 'temporary civil servant' added. Nothing was being given away. It was only from outside Oxford that C. F. Beckingham, whom I knew in BP, expanded this reference to read 'seconded for service with military and naval Intelligence, 1942–6'.

I was never as conscious in post-1946 Oxford, as I was in post-war Cambridge, that I was in a university that had shaped BP. I knew that Denniston had recruited the mathematician Peter Twinn from Brasenose College before the beginning of the war, but I knew too that when Twinn was interviewed for five minutes by Dilly Knox before joining GC&CS, Oxford was not once mentioned. All that Twinn remembered of the interview was that Knox made it clear that he did not care much for mathematicians.

Trevor-Roper himself was encouraged from above to write a book in 1968, *The Philby Affair: Espionage, Treason and Secret Services*, in which he still had nothing good to say about SIS. He went so far as to call its contribution to the war effort an 'irrelevancy', a judgement which the authorized historian of SIS, Keith Jeffery, describes as 'preposterous'. What Trevor-Roper wrote about Philby in his book of 1968, based largely on articles that he had published previously in *Encounter* (with a piece added on Canaris), was very well expressed and very much to the point.

Philby had published his book *My Silent War* in the same year with a eulogistic introduction by Graham Greene, which to Trevor-Roper had an element of the 'absurd' about it. Trevor-Roper's own book was in his own words 'in part at least a by-product of my experience in the War of 1939 to 1945'. He had met Philby for the first time in 1941, when they were both in SIS, and found him congenial company, 'undeniably competent, the most competent and industrious man in a generally lax organisation', but their lives diverged after D-Day.

It is of continuing interest, as Trevor-Roper pointed out, that within SIS Philby was regarded as 'the man of the future', a candidate for the headship of SIS itself after Menzies. GC&CS would then have been under his supervision. Trevor-Roper did not dwell on what might have happened. Unlike Hinsley, he had no brief for so-called counter-factual history. Instead he laid total stress on Philby's remarkable duplicity. Every statement that Philby made, including the summary of his own life in *My Silent War*, was 'nicely calculated in advance by his masters in the KGB'.

Summaries of the lives of all the people working inside BP do not raise such profound matters of judgement. With the exception of Cairncross, who did not like most of the people that Philby or, indeed Trevor-Roper, liked, Bletchley lives carried no hint of treachery. When Philby read the cryptic words 'Foreign Office' in the entries the Oxford dons wrote in *Who's Who* he would have been amused. For the dons described in this chapter it was appropriately vague to cover a multiplicity of possibilities.

It was not only Oxford (or Cambridge) dons who figure in the history of BP and of intelligence. Undergraduates and graduates of colleges, who would never see their names in *Who's Who*, must find their place in the BP scenario. Among them women, who always constituted a majority in BP and were always a minority in Oxford, deserve to have their lives recalled. The women's college in Oxford that has done most to do justice to them is Lady Margaret Hall whose graduates have told their own stories.

Among the LMH graduates is my friend Ann Mitchell, like me a survivor, who is as knowledgeable as I am of – and as interested in – the last two years of Hut Six. She was one of only five LMH women who were accepted for BP for interviews after being recommended for BP, in her case after an interview by the Oxford Appointments Board. Her post had no job description: she was appointed a temporary assistant in the Foreign Office at a salary of £150 a year, to be increased to £200 when she reached the age of twenty-one after a few months. Placed in the Machine Room next to the Watch, she found that most of the women on her first shift were, like her, mathematicians, augmented by a number of economists. Years after the war she discovered that one of her colleagues, a mathematics teacher who sorted out 'dud' messages, was the sister of the Sherborne schoolmaster who taught Turing.

Ann 'bumped into' many people from Oxford inside BP and in the surrounding villages where they were billeted, and in 2010 she was to visit the Park, not for the first time since the war, with a party from her college. Had she been older and an undergraduate there under the previous principal of Lady Margaret Hall, Lynda Grier, it might have been her principal and not the Oxford Appointments Board that directed her to Bletchley. Just before the war began Jocelyn Bostock, a recent LMH graduate, asked Grier to put forward her name for BP, and Grier, the one head of a women's college to appeal to Worcester's Dean Wilkinson, duly obeyed. Jocelyn was, therefore, one of the first women recruits to join BP, and designated, as Ann was, a Foreign Office Temporary Assistant, she became a highly valued assistant to Hinsley in Hut Four.

Lynda Grier had her own Bletchley links. The day Jocelyn approached her she had had a letter from Denniston's wife asking whether LMH could recommend some German speakers to join BP and according to Jocelyn she named six. In 1941 she supplied five, including Elizabeth Taylor, who read German and was interviewed in BP by Josh Cooper and Arthur (Bill) Bonsall who was to become head of GCHQ in the 1970s.

Jocelyn's future husband, whom she had met in Oxford and who was in the Army serving abroad, visited Bletchley several times before they were married in 1942, but of course he was never allowed in the Park. He shared for a time, however, the pub outside Bletchley that was frequented by Turing and they got on well, with Turing telling him that he would like to recruit him for Hut Eight but could not recruit people in the Army. Before her marriage Jocelyn met a girl from Somerville College, Hilary Brett, working in Hut Eight with Turing. Hinsley subsequently married her. Did they ever tell each other their secrets?

Later recruits from LMH included Elizabeth Davies and Félicité Berryman, both of whom, varying the pattern, had been sent down from the college. Rachel Makover varied the pattern in a different way. She went straight to BP from Roedean School and went up to LMH only in 1948. At BP she worked in Hut Seven, concerned with the breaking of Japanese naval codes, in her case the so-called Fisherman's code (a merchant navy liason cypher) , JN-40, which to her delight she once broke before the Americans did. Her BP grade on entry was a grade III clerk, and the highest grade of clerk to which she could rise was II.

She knew that her father was an officer in the Intelligence Corps, serving in North Africa, where he had won the Military Cross, but was surprised one day when she was called into a BP office and told that her father was flying into Northolt with 'something for Bletchley' and asked whether she would like to go and meet him. She had last seen him when she was thirteen. When she went up to LMH in 1948 she found herself reading English with an ex-ATS girl who had been a Y Service interceptor, who had learnt to read Morse at the impressive speed of 27 words per minute. She had done some of her training in Trowbridge.

No other Oxford women's college has provided such a detailed record of its BP connections. There were, however, two colleges in Oxford, St Antony's, brand new in 1950, and Mansfield, a non-conformist establishment, not then treated as a college of the university, whose members knew a little about the BP story. The first Warden of St Antony's, William (Bill) Deakin, had headed the British Military Mission to Tito in 1943 and was first secretary in the British Embassy in Belgrade from 1945 to 1946. He was as close to Churchill as Menzies. Mansfield College was essentially a part of GC&CS. It dealt with the production of British codes and cyphers and their security, then part of the remit of GC&CS.

A reason sometimes given for placing this work in Mansfield was said to be its closeness to the Oxford University Press. I never accepted that. Given the pressure on space inside BP, care of British cyphers remained concentrated in Mansfield until 1946 when the people working there were transferred to GCHQ. I never knew anything of this change of role when I was a fellow of Worcester College. I did know, however, that one non-collegiate institution in Oxford, the Institute of Statistics, where at least one ex-BPite, Kenneth Knowles, worked, reproduced, in part at least, the open, experimental and superficially rankless flavour of BP. Certainly there were mathematicians working there of the kind that BP always took to its heart.

## Chapter 10

# The Bletchley Trust

I visited BP only once in the first five years after the war ended. I was on my way from Oxford to Cambridge by train, and I got out at Bletchley station to wander through what I thought of as the village of Bletchley to find out what had happened to it after I left. Before I had time to get beyond the station exit I was stopped by an impressive man in uniform who asked me if I was reporting for 'the course'. I wish now that I had said yes. I should have discovered what the course was about and found my way in un-accompanied. Clearly there was a lot of activity inside the Park, much of it concerned – or so it seemed – with communications. Obviously much had happened after Barbara Abernethy locked the gates of the Park and took the keys down to Eastcote in 1946.

I learned that the General Post Office, after all its wartime connections with GC&CS, was now the largest peacetime user of BP, employing Block H as a training centre for telephone exchange operators and maintenance engineers and as a place to demonstrate new types of telephone and teleprinter equipment. In 1968 it was to erect a new building, Faulkner House, which incorporated lots of glass, a material that could not have been employed on any scale in the wartime blocks. The Mansion was used for offices and meetings of senior executives.

It was many years later that I learned that the first people to return to BP – very appropriately – had been displaced Poles who would not or could not return to Communist Poland. They were housed in Blocks A, B and E in 1946. The last of them had not left until early in 1949. Meanwhile, the Control Commission for Germany, which many wartime BPites had joined, took over several vacant buildings, including huts, late in 1946. Known as the Foreign Office Training Wing, the Commission stayed there until late 1947.

By a curious twist of fortune GCHQ returned to BP early in 1948 and took over parts of Block D and almost the whole of Block C for a Central Training School. It was followed in 1948 by the Ministry of Aviation which acquired six wings of Block D and a small corner of Block C. These were used to teach airport ground staff how to communicate with aircraft and to work with instrument landing systems and radar. That would doubtless have been the most interesting course for me to follow if I had told the man who met me at Bletchley Station that I was reporting for one.

For many old BPites the most congenial course would have been that designed by the Special Communications Unit of MI6, Section 8, re-named the Diplomatic Wireless Service, which was located from the summer of 1949 in Huts Three and Eight. There was some social cooperation, if limited, between the Diplomatic Wireless Service and the other users of post-war BP, though whether they were keeping secret from each other what they were doing I do not know. In 1948 Hut Four became a social club and dining area which the users shared, but the GPO maintained a sports and social club of its own in the old Hut Nine.

As in the past, GCHQ, growing in numbers, found that the space available for its work in the Park had become inadequate, and as a result it acquired a large field north of BP later to be named Furzton. A radio direction finding system developed by the

Germans was installed there. Judged superior to all existing British systems, it consisted of an outer circle of forty and an inner circle of thirty smaller metal masts. It proved more and more difficult, however, for any section of GCHQ to remain in BP after the railway line to London was electrified in the 1960s, and eventually all of its Bletchley operations were moved far away to Culmhead in Somerset.

Perhaps the most successful post-war venture in BP was a teacher training college, set up at a time when there was a severe shortage of teachers. Created in January 1948 after the displaced Poles had mostly left Bletchley, it took over the remains of Elmers School, many of the empty wartime huts and three blocks, A, B and E. Finally in 1957 a large assembly hall was opened by Princess Alexandra in what had been BP's wartime teleprinter room. Local newspapers described the occasion as the first visit to Bletchley of any member of the royal family, and there were no references whatever in the local press to the wartime role of BP. For almost another twenty years this was to remain shrouded in secrecy. The veil was at last being lifted in 1976 when, as part of a large-scale reorganization of teacher training, the college ceased to exist, and the Ministry of Aviation, now re-named the Civil Aviation Authority, moved into Blocks A, B and E.

The 1970s was not only a decade of disclosure of wartime intelligence secrets, still limited, but of a widely aired and far-reaching reorganization of inherited institutions, including local government and communications agencies. Reorganization of the former had an immediate impact. Bletchley, previously run as an urban district council, now became part of Milton Keynes, a new town with an old name, the name of a village which now became part of it. Communications influenced its choice as a new town created under the New Towns Act of 1946 as they had influenced the choice of wartime BP, but these had already changed after the building of Britain's first motorway, the M1.

Soon there was to be a 'contemporary-looking' new station, opened, I believe, by the Prince of Wales, that contrasted totally with the Bletchley station that all BPites knew. Trains rushed through it as they had rushed through wartime Bletchley, some stopping there. Cars were now far more important than they had been during the war, in years of petrol rationing and closed and unsignposted roads. It was they that dictated the grid-design layout of the new Milton Keynes with its multiplicity of roundabouts. It was praised by the architectural historian Rayner Banham as a model for the rest of the world. Milton Keynes also included Newport Pagnell, a town where several wartime BPites lived, the most agreeable place for a billet.

The new town became a unitary authority in 1997. It now had a population of 170,000 and was split into two parliamentary constituencies, north-east and south-west, the latter incorporating Bletchley. The MP for Milton Keynes South-West until 2010, Phyllis Starkey, who took a great interest in the restoration of BP, was one of the councillors for my local ward in Oxford when I was provost of Worcester College.

On the same day as the Prince of Wales opened the new station, he also visited the recently founded Open University, which had been located in Milton Keynes largely because the Milton Keynes Development Corporation was keen that the new town should have a new university. A site for it was offered on very favourable terms at an old hall, Walton Hall, where BPites had lived and worked during the war. The architects chosen in 1969 to design its buildings, Max Fry and Jane Drew, both well-known to me, offered to produce in time for the university's opening and the taking in of its first students in 1971, a block of 'permanent' university buildings rather than temporary premises. No huts!

Further testimony to the reorganization and development theme of the 1970s was the national change of name and function of the General Post Office which, in the same year as Fry and Drew were appointed, ceased to be a government department and became a corporation. In 1981 its activities were divided into two with telecommunications being administered separately from postal and banking services. In 1984 the corporation managing telecommunications services was given a new name, British Telecom.

Within a rapidly changing local and national scene BP was in an increasingly run-down condition during the 1970s and 1980s. Problems had started earlier when the remains of Elmers School were deliberately set on fire and its surviving interior gutted in 1969. More seriously, parts of the Mansion, such as the old ballroom, were semi-derelict and easily vandalized during the 1970s, and in 1986–7 BT, now more familiar in initials than BP, demolished the whole of Block F, itself an act of vandalism. Nothing was now being spent on maintenance, and finally BT, no longer willing to retain any of its buildings at Bletchley, went on to close Block G, Faulkner House and two tower blocks it had built for accommodation for students.

Closing a long period of history, BT had already got rid of Dollis Hill, where Tommy Flowers and his team had worked with relentless intensity on Colossus. On that site there were now expensive private apartments. BT moved from BP to purpose-built offices in Kents Hill on the eastern side of Milton Keynes, and it now seemed likely that the whole of what was left of BP would be bulldozed. There were echoes of 1937: residential housing was considered the best answer for the BP estate. This was the clearly expressed view of the government properties agency PACE, Property Advisers to the Civil Estate, which owned BP with BT as tenants.

It was in these deeply disturbing circumstances that the Bletchley Archaeological and Historical Society intervened in the BP story – only just in time, as Captain Ridley's 'Shooting Party' had been only just in time in 1938. Sue Jarvis, who had moved to Bletchley in 1961, organized the crucial meeting of the Society, of which she was a founder member, in her front room over tea. She lived within 300 yards of the front gate of the Park.

The Society stressed that it wanted not only to welcome back to the site old BPites, sometimes now called 'Parkees' or more simply 'veterans', but the 'general public', largely ignorant of what they would find there, but curious to have a glimpse of what to them was now quite distant history. What would become the Trust would not just be a museum or a group of museums. It would acquire and preserve 'documents, photographs, recordings, paintings, drawings and artefacts', provide lectures and seminars and publish 'books, leaflets, films, videos, recordings and pictures'.

Before it was formally incorporated on 7 July 1992 as a trust, a charitable company limited by guarantee and having no share capital, a reunion of enthusiastic 'veterans' was held on 19 October 1991, which about 400 attended. There had been previous reunions since the 1950s, some of them restricted to people in particular huts, like Hut Six, not all of them held in BP itself. The Trust proposed more regular reunions for old BPites of all kinds, including among them men and women who had worked not at BP itself but in BP's out-stations and in the Y Service. They, in particular, felt that their wartime efforts, which had helped to win the war, had been totally neglected. There was still little public knowledge of wartime BP in the country as a whole, but the demand secured valuable local backing from stalwarts like Peter Wescombe and Peter Jarvis, a doctor and medical director of local community hospitals.

What gave most encouragement to the trustees was the knowledge that large numbers of volunteers who could not remember wartime BP were prepared to devote their efforts to opening up the site, which in February 1992 was designated a Conservation Area, with the Mansion and the stableyard buildings listed as Grade 1. Two notable recruits to the Trust were Tony Sale and Ted Enever, volunteers who were prepared to dedicate a large part of their time to the affairs of a renovated BP. They were disappointed that the already historic wartime buildings in BP, huts and blocks, the places where most of the work of BP had been carried on, were rejected for any kind of listing in 1993.

Since 1993 the Bletchley Park Trust has had a history longer than that of wartime BP, a history not free from friction and faction, but going through as many distinct phases as the secret Bletchley days covered in my book. I first discussed its formation with my friend Sir Edward Tompkins, former diplomat, who lived in a wonderful manor house in Winslow, one of the most beautiful houses (and gardens) in Buckinghamshire that I have ever seen. It was he, the oldest member of the trustees, who kept a careful eye on the sometimes tangled affairs of the early Trust. The man who soon became chairman, another prominent local landowner, Sir Philip Duncombe, born in Great Brickhill, gave him confidence in the future of BP. I was sad that because of frequent visits abroad and subsequently illnesses I could not be of more help.

The five years after December 1993, the month when the last people working on the site for the Civil Aviation Authority, then chaired by Christopher Chataway, finally left it, were years when the future of BP continued to rest largely on dedicated volunteers. They carried out all manner of tasks from posting leaflets about the Park under car windscreen wipers and serving as guides, to keeping the buildings and grounds in order, and, not least, catering and washing up in the canteen. They staged the first exhibition in Block A in 1994, showing an Enigma machine, a Lorenz machine and a Churchill bust, closing at 4.30 p.m. and taking back the precious objects to be stored in the vault of the Mansion.

Fortunately it was not only individuals who volunteered. 'Groups', consisting of diverse voluntary associations and societies formed a Groups Committee, chaired by Mark Cornelius, who himself exhibited a toy and memorabilia collection. John Chapman and his group ran a Bletchley Park Post Office. Margaret Sale, Tony Sale's wife, was ubiquitous. Despite all their efforts, the morale of the volunteers was said to be low in 1998, for the trustees were divided, and PACE and BT's director of property had lost patience in negotiating with them on a new lease for the core area of BP which the Trust would manage, with the rest of the site being left for other uses. Roger Bristow, chief executive of the Trust, resigned and there was a last blow when the BP site was not picked out for a shortlist of UNESCO World Heritage sites.

The climax of this first period in the history of the Trust, almost as long in itself as the Second World War, was the filming of a widely praised television programme for Channel 4, *Station X*. The enthusiastic young crew, none of whom remembered the war, filmed their programme inside and outside BP, including at my own home in Lewes. They learned much in the process. For Duncombe the highlight of his chairmanship was the visit of Polish dignitaries in 1999 marking the sixtieth anniversary of the Polish handing over of Enigma machines to the British in 1939.

In January 1998 a newly constituted executive committee of the Trust held its first meeting and decided to appoint a trust director who would have a new remit, and in February 1998 Christine Large, known to most of the trustees as a BP volunteer, was appointed for a nine-month period with strong outside support from, among others, John Walker, chief executive of the Commission for New Towns. However, her appointment was in face of vocal inside opposition, particularly from Sale, who was Museums Director as well as a trustee, and his wife who had an office in the Mansion and kept the keys. Christine herself complained that nine months was far too short a period to accomplish what she wished to do and what she considered essential for the future of BP.

The then top priority in her strategic plan was the acquisition of the maximum core site that was possible through a deal with PACE and BT; a second priority was a 'regeneration' of that core site of the Park to assist the realization of the full potential not only of the historic site but of a depressed Bletchley within the Milton Keynes area. The third priority was to give a new impetus to the development of BP's 'heritage assets'. At a full board meeting in May 1998 she reported that she had received a grant of £8,000 from the Commission for New Towns to enable a reformed Trust to produce a development brief and a strategic and business plan, and in June she presented what she had written to PACE and BT.

There was further delay, but her contract was extended, and she went on to propose changes in the structure of the Trust, including the setting up of a management and planning team and in March 1999 at the annual general meeting of the Trust its mission was succinctly reaffirmed and extended:

> To achieve a living memorial to World War II Intelligence work, computing and cryptography, through the creation of an integrated heritage park of international repute. With an overall theme of the science of communications, the Park will comprise four zones: covering heritage, conference, community and knowledge.

Unfortunately, the mission statement did not dispel tension, even conflict, within the ranks of the trustees, some of whom paid little attention to the warnings of Chris Smith, their highly responsible finance director, of the serious financial consequences of their relentless opposition. There were ironical echoes in all this of the personal disputes in wartime Hut Three before Eric Jones took over. A new factor, however, was that there were leaks to the press, which would not have been possible during the war.

Nevertheless, in June 1999 an agreement for a lease was at last signed by representatives of the Secretary of State for the Environment, BT and the chairman of the trustees, and in 2001 a new board of trustees was brought into existence under the chairmanship of Christopher Chataway, politician, businessman and champion runner, who had been told in 1991 by Air Vice-Marshal John Browne, who had been involved with him in the Civil Aviation Authority, that when the time was right he should lead a new trust to save BP. He had an interesting link too with wartime BP. As a schoolboy he had trained at a running track belonging to the Walton Athletic Club where Turing too had trained as a marathon runner.

In the new board Browne became a trustee. So, too, did Evelyn de Rothschild, one of Britain's best-known merchant bankers, and the distinguished judge Sir Oliver Popplewell. Chataway's vice-chairman was Martin Findlay, an active figure in the world of corporate business. It was an extra asset that he and Rothschild lived close by, as Duncombe had done. One new trustee, whom I personally recommended, was Roy McLaren, the Canadian high commissioner, who was totally outside the fray.

Among the BP 'veterans' drawn into the affairs of the Trust in 2003 was Baroness Trumpington, who had joined Hut Four in 1940 as Jean Campbell-Harris. In 2003, when she made a speech at the opening of the new visitor information centre, Hut Four had become a place where you could have a drink at the bar. Now Jean could place its history in perspective.

She had been introduced to BP by Frank Birch, who offered her a place as a cypher clerk after meeting her at a Lyons corner house in London, a favourite wartime rendezvous. When she arrived in BP in 1940 there were 400 people working there. When she left there were thousands. She had been back to BP twice between the end of the war and 2003, on the second occasion to celebrate the fiftieth anniversary of VJ-Day in 1995. Her message in 2003 was that the visitor centre was exactly what was needed to help present and future visitors to appreciate 'the special part played by all of us, the very great and the very insignificant, towards the winning of the Second World War'.

That was a long-term view, and Jean was exactly the right person to present it in twenty-first century BP. Likewise the Duke of Kent, the royal patron of BP, was exactly the right person to open the Bletchley Park Story in the first phase of the National Codes Centre's new exhibition complex in Block B, overlooking the lake. A royal visit souvenir issue of the *Friends of Bletchley Park Newsletter* was printed for the occasion. On display for the first time was a piece of the original Colossus. The exhibition began with a timeline and incorporated an interactive display of a German U-boat Enigma station, a Y Service radio listening station and a four-rotor Enigma machine. There was also a children's cartoon history of BP. 'You have been an outstanding patron over the years,' Christopher Chataway told the Duke. 'We are delighted you are here today to see what has been achieved. It is an extremely important story to tell.'

Later, in the summer of 2004, an American garden trail was opened at BP to commemorate the special relationship between the UK and the USA developed during the war with the 1943 BRUSA accords. The garden trail started at the giant sequoia tree planted by the Leon family and led around the lake. Mavis Batey, garden historian as well as cryptographer, played an important part in opening up the trail. On 11 September a Churchill weekend was held in the Park, and a week later an Enigma and Family festival and an Enigma reunion.

At the beginning of October 2005, after lengthy discussion with the conservation officer of Milton Keynes Council and English Heritage, work started on the restoration of Hut Eight. The work involved the stripping out of all the kitchen and electrical equipment installed when the Civil Aviation Authority used the hut as a canteen and the construction of new partitions in the original partition positions. It would take six months to complete and the hut would reopen with an exhibition recalling the capture of Enigma secrets from *U-559*.

It was announced in the *Bletchley Park Newsletter* for winter 2005 that there was now a Bletchley Park Heritage Panel chaired by Sir Richard Dearlove, master of Pembroke College, Cambridge, who had joined SIS in1966, and had become its chief, C, in 1999. Founder members of the panel included David Kahn, who has figured prominently throughout this book, and Jack Copeland, professor of philosophy at Canterbury , New Zealand, who, as is noted in this chapter, is director of the Turing Archive for the

History of Computing, and who gave the first Turing Memorial Lecture in 2005.

In the same number of the *Newsletter* tributes were paid to the Reverend Maurice Wiles, Regius Professor of Divinity in the University of Oxford. I knew him when he was at BP during the war when he deferred an open scholarship he had been awarded by Christ's College, Cambridge. After Pearl Harbor he was recruited to take the remarkable rapid course in Japanese at Bedford and then moved on to BP to work on various Japanese cyphers. Another obituary noted in the same number was that of Albert Leslie Yoxall, an alumnus of my own college. In June of that year we had a Sidney Sussex Society visit to BP organized by Peter Lipscombe. I was invited to the gathering and spoke openly for the first time of what I had done there during the war. John Herivel should have spoken with me, but he had fallen off his bicycle in Oxford and couldn't join us.

To me the most interesting item in the *Newsletter* for winter 2005 was an announcement of a brand-new course in cryptology which had been held at Marlborough College, which remains prominent in all my memories of Hut Six. The course was taught by Harry Beckhough, a wartime cryptographer, who was then 91 'and still going strong'. There was no reference, however, to the current teaching staff of the college, including its mathematicians. A year earlier a high-level course on 'Security: the New Enigmas' had been held at BP in conjunction with the Open University and other partners, focussing on the implications for society as a whole of the choices surrounding the use of the internet and cyber responsibility. In 2010 the University of Buckingham was to advertise a degree course for 'people interested in the history of intelligence', dealing with current issues of intelligence and security.

In the autumn of 2005 Christopher Chataway announced that Christine Large would stay on as director of the Trust until the end of 2006. In spring 2006, however, having secured a new post, she handed over the directorship to Simon Greenish, leaving behind her a new exhibition and interpretation plan. The spring issue of BP's *Newsletter* ends with the words, 'This is my farewell edition of the *Newsletter*. May you and Bletchley Park continue to thrive.' Among her recent achievements Chataway listed the inauguration of the Bletchley Park Science and Innovation Centre, opened by Lord Sainsbury, the minister responsible for UK Science plc. Its refurbishment was to be completed in 2006. Its clients included Cerevision, concerned with lighting and display technology; IP Cortex, a specialist telecoms and IT solutions provider; IProof, managing IT security and digital rights; UK Displays Network, a government-backed hub of display technology; MLG, a European consultancy; Createonline, an internet-based image-management and print-on-demand service; and Central Innovation Network, linking technologists, entrepreneurs and investors in the Milton Keynes area. Great emphasis was to be placed in the future on job creation for the whole area. English Partnerships, the national regeneration agency, reached agreement with the Office for Government Commerce, British Telecom, and the BP Trust on the take-over of the Forces Military Vehicles site inside BP, the site of the former Block F, and a ten-year lease of Block D.

A new and exciting period in the history of the BP Trust began in May 2006 when Simon Greenish took over as director. There was a link with the post-war past described in the first part of this chapter for Greenish had stayed in the Park when he took part in a course put on by the Civil Aviation Authority for which he was then working. That was a link with Christopher Chataway too.

His first task in a series of inter-related tasks was to raise necessary funds to meet running costs, and he accomplished that by the summer of 2007. The budget was balanced. Visitor numbers as well as income were both up in that year.

His other tasks were further to develop and improve museum presentation, including the Enigma Museum and the National Computer Museum; to strengthen the role of BP in the Milton Keynes local community; and, most important of all, to plan for the long-term future of the Park. An important element in that was the restoration of Huts Six and Three, the two Huts with which I was most intimately involved during the war years.

To accomplish these tasks BP had to broaden its contacts and to change its style. In particular, there had to be a more positive and focused approach to marketing and to publicity. Greenish set out his plans in a new publication which was far more than an in-house journal, the *Bletchley Park Times*, which appeared twice a year. He found exactly the right man to edit it, Philip Le Grand, a graduate of the University of Cardiff in 1983 with a degree in physics, computing and electronics, with subsequent years in business, who volunteered to take it on, choosing its name and shaping its content and setting out deliberately and imaginatively to broaden its appeal. Le Grand had figured with his son Jonathan in an article in the former *Friends' Newsletter* in winter 2006, when he was volunteering for duties in the Park, meeting and greeting visitors.

The Friends of Bletchley Park had printed a newsletter since 2003, which I read regularly and which has provided me with invaluable information for this book, but the *Bletchley Park Times* was to do something different. In the words of Le Grand it would 'reflect the various times or ages of Bletchley Park – Past, Present and Future'.

The past seemed straightforward: people who had worked in BP sent in pieces about themselves and asked about old BPites. A fuller picture was painted than ever before. The in-tray was always full. The present was alive: there was usually news to report. The future was uncertain: funds were needed 'in every corner' if BP was to be preserved and developed into a 'world-class heritage site'. Greenish and Le Grand were of one mind and one will and they both appreciated the value of media interest in the Park and the publication of stories about it. In the spring 2009 issue of *Bletchley Park Times* Greenish commended and thanked Le Grand for all the work he was putting into the publication. Feedback was always positive.

Meanwhile, he went on, 'we have continued to achieve very high levels of excellent publicity, with visits from MPs and other well-known personalities, the most recent being Stephen Fry. This attention has undoubtedly increased public awareness of the Park.' There would be a slight re-design of the *Bletchley Park Times*, he went on, 'to make the magazine more commercial so that it can go on sale, as well as providing it for the Friends'. It was more than slight. The by then old cover had incorporated several 'items of Bletchley Park, including the Mansion, the goose that laid the Golden Eggs, a Bombe menu and rotor, and paper tape used by Colossus'. In the autumn of 2009 it gave way to a new cover with a whole page illustration and a headline printed in block capitals, 'The Griffins Return'. There were griffins outside the old Mansion before the arrival of Captain Ridley's 'Shooting Party'.

The new griffins, unveiled by Stephen Fry, were created by stone-cutter Michelle Brown. In this issue two pages were devoted, however, to 'heritage plans'. Space was given to the story of the commitment to the Park of Sue Black, head of the Department of

Information and Software Systems in the School of Electronic and Computer Science at the University of Westminster. She had visited BP for the first time in 2003 for a meeting of the British Computer Society, held in the Mansion, and met a project team led by John Harper, which had been working on the rebuilding of a bombe. Until she first went to BP she had no idea of how many women had worked there and at its out-stations during the war. She secured funds from the British Computer Society and the UK Resource Centre for Women in Science, Engineering and Technology to carry out a small-scale project on their contribution to the war effort.

Deeply concerned with the financial problems of BP as a whole, she emailed all professors and heads of computer science departments in the United Kingdom, finding out at once how many of them had already signed a petition to save BP which was active on the 10 Downing Street website. With John Turner she wrote a letter to *The Times* which was signed by no fewer than ninety-seven of them. She also publicized what she was doing on the Radio 4 *Today* programme and on BBC Television, starting a blog and, in December 2008, a Twitter campaign which brought in Stephen Fry. In September 2009 the Heritage Lottery Fund offered the Park £460,000, with a possible £4 million to follow. This was the biggest transformation of the finances of BP since the setting up of the Trust, but, as Simon Greenish pointed out, it was the beginning of a process, not its culmination. The person who had known this difference best was Winston Churchill.

The modes of communication are totally different now from what they were in Churchill's long life. An article in the *Bletchley Park Times* for autumn 2009 admirably summarized the latest of them. Key developments had been miniaturization, portability, de-regulation of the spectrum, mobile telephones, and social networking. I have traced the most important of these with Peter Burke in our *Social History of the Media, From Gutenberg to the Internet*, which has gone through four editions since it first appeared in 2002 and has been published in more than twenty languages.

Yet there has been continuity as well as contrast in the story, and one of the most memorable events of 2009 was the 'Wireless Waves' gathering in August, where bodies like the Bletchley Park Radio Society and Milton Keynes Amateur Radio Society, neither of which existed during the war, exhibited equipment going back before 1939. There is a thriving Vintage and Military Amateur Radio Society. Meanwhile the Radio Society of Great Britain, founded before the First World War, formally expresses institutional continuity.

There was impressive growth in 2010. On 25 March the Minister for Culture, Media and Sport, Ben Bradshaw, announced on a visit to BP that a grant of £250,000 would be made to the Trust out of re-allocated departmental underspends. As an ongoing site, BP would now be able to resurface badly pot-holed roads and car parks, repair the leaking roof of Block A and carry out maintenance on other buildings. This sign that the government recognized the importance of BP as a national site gave a boost to a BP very different from the BP of a few years before. Bradshaw nevertheless went back in time in announcing the intention behind the grant: 'The work carried out at Bletchley Park had a huge impact on the course of the war.' Following on after the successful bid for a first phase of funding from the Heritage Lottery Fund in 2009, Heritage Education went even further back in time and memorably described BP as being as symbolic for the 'Information Age' as Ironbridge was for the 'Industrial Revolution'. Having written a book on Ironbridge, I welcomed this parallel.

I also welcomed the emphasis placed by the Trust on education at all levels, a preoccupation too of the present-day Ironbridge Museum. Children specializing in information and communications technology had their visits arranged from the beginning of 2010 onwards by the National Computer Museum. The rest had a variety of interests. In the academic year 2002–3, fifty-four schools had arranged visits to BP. In 2009 there were 6,628 school visitors, in 2010 6,811. In 2010 BP received a coveted Learning Outside the Classroom quality badge. One of the activities singled out in that year was 'Secret Science', which relates directly to the title of this book. 'We try to make the most of our "Top Secret" reputation,' the organizers stated, 'to inspire children during their activities.'

It is praiseworthy perhaps that secrecy is now a game not an obligation. There are still secrets of BP that are not being released. The official history of Hut Six prepared at the end of the war, on which I have drawn heavily in this book, was de-classified as late as June 2006, and the technical volume that accompanied it remains in oblivion. In June 2010 it was announced that an agreement had been reached with Hewlett Packard to digitize BP's surprisingly large wartime archive. The initial phase of digitization was to take a year or more. The only individuals mentioned were Alan Turing and, out of the blue, Ian Fleming.

Within BP Turing had always been *the* iconic figure since the Trust was founded in 1991. In 2005 a rich and enterprising American businessman and benefactor, Sidney E. Frank, famous for his Grey Goose vodka and a champion of Turing, had supported BP's plans to add a new science wing to its National Codes Centre in Block B at the entrance to the Park, and Jack Copeland had given the first Turing Memorial Lecture in the ballroom of the Mansion. Several members of the Turing family were present. Copeland had exactly the right credentials to deliver this lecture on Turing and Artificial Intelligence. In the same year he wrote a book. *The Essential Turing: The Ideas that Gave Birth to the Computer Age.* In 2006 he was to edit *Colossus: The Secrets of Bletchley Park's Code-breaking Computers.*

In almost every number of the *Bletchley Park Times*, there is new information about Turing and articles devoted to his multi-faceted work. The greatest tribute to him in BP, however, is the building of a new Colossus. Tony Sale has been behind this un-precedented venture, and the new Colossus, visible to the visiting public, is BP's greatest attraction.

Alan Turing was born in 1912, and 2012 is being planned as Alan Turing Year. There has been an inspiring lead into it. In February 2011 a collection of Max Newman's hand-annotated offprints from sixteen of Turing's eighteen books and papers were purchased by the Trust with help from the National Heritage Memorial Fund and a donation of $100,000 from Google. The papers were up for auction and had they not been bought by the Trust they likely would have gone to a private collector or, worse, have been split up. They will now be available to the public at the Bletchley Park Museum. This is more than a historical collection: it is a tribute to all the changes that have taken place in the world of communications since the introduction of the internet and the worldwide web. BP is now on a world map. Meanwhile interest in the remarkable personality of Turing continues to grow everywhere.

## Appendix

# Selective Chronology

| Date | Historical events | Intelligence and Cryptography |
| --- | --- | --- |
| 1909 | | |
| | | Beginnings of the British secret services, MI5 and MI6 |
| 1914 | | |
| Aug | First World War starts | Room 40 in the Admiralty |
| 1917 | | |
| 6 Apr | United States goes to war | |
| 1918 | | |
| Feb | Treaty of Brest-Litovsk (Russia, Germany) | Scherbius files patent for Enigma cypher machine |
| 11 Nov | Armistice Day | |
| 1919 | Treaty of Versailles Covenant of the League of Nations | Government Code and Cypher School (GC&CS) established |
| 1921 | Hitler becomes Führer of Nazi Party | |
| 1923 | | Enigma machine exhibited at International Postal Union Congress, Switzerland |
| 1926 | General Strike in Britain | German Navy begins to use an early model of Enigma machine |
| 1928 | | Germany Army begins to use Enigma |

| 1929 | Wall Street financial crash | US Army Signals Intelligence Service 'Black Chamber' shut down |
|---|---|---|
| 1931 | National Government in Britain | |
| 1932 | | Schmidt betrays Enigma secrets to the French; they pass them to the Poles who go on to break Enigma |
| 1933 | F. D. Roosevelt becomes President of USA<br>Hitler becomes Chancellor of Germany | |
| 1934 | Revival of German Luftwaffe | |
| 1936 | German reoccupation of the Rhineland<br>Axis Alliance between Germany and Italy<br>Spanish Civil War begins | |
| 1937 | Chamberlain becomes Prime Minister | |

**1938**

| | | |
|---|---|---|
| *Mar* | Hitler annexes Austria | |
| *Sept* | Munich Agreement | |
| *Nov* | | New indicator system for German Army Enigma |

**1939**

| | | |
|---|---|---|
| *Mar* | Germany occupies Bohemia and Moravia; Britain and France offer support to Poland | |
| *June* | End of Spanish Civil War | New Japanese naval code, JN-25 |
| *July* | | Poles reveal their Enigma successes to Britain and France |
| *21 Aug* | Nazi–Soviet pact | |
| *1 Sept* | Germany invades Poland | |

| | | |
|---|---|---|
| 3 Sept | Britain and France declare war | |
| **1940** | | |
| Jan | | First BP break into Enigma using hand methods |
| Feb | | British obtain two of three unknown rotors used in Naval Enigma from *U-33* |
| Mar | | First experimental Turing bombe delivered to BP |
| 9 Apr | Germany invades Denmark and Norway | |
| 1 May | | Luftwaffe and Heer stop double-encyphering message settings |
| 10 May | Germany attacks Netherlands and Belgium; Churchill becomes Prime Minister | |
| May | | First BP break into wartime Naval Enigma through captured papers |
| 22 May | | BP begins to break Red key again |
| 26 May | Dunkirk evacuation begins | |
| 10 June | Italy declares war | |
| 22 June | France capitulates | |
| 10 July | Air Battle of Britain begins | |
| 8 Aug | | Bombe No. 2 with diagonal board introduced |
| Sept | | Purple first broken by US Army; first JN-25 decrypts by OP-20-G |
| 13 Sept | Italy invades Egypt | |
| 15 Sept | Hitler postpones invasion of Britain | |
| 20 Oct | | Escaped Polish cryptographers resume cypher work in France |
| 28 Oct | Italy invades Greece | |
| Nov | | BP breaks Brown key used by Luftwaffe to set up navigation beams |

| | | |
|---|---|---|
| *Dec* | British throw Italians out of Egypt | BP breaks main Abwehr hand cypher |
| **1941** | | |
| *Jan–Mar* | | Two bombes delivered to BP, one the first Jumbo |
| *28 Jan* | | Luftwaffe operational key for North Africa broken |
| *2 Feb* | | US Army and Navy crypto-graphers visit BP and give BP copies of Japanese Purple cypher machine |
| *7 Feb* | | German railway Enigma broken |
| *8 Feb* | | BP breaks German meteoro-logical hand cypher |
| *Mar* | | Naval Enigma messages read |
| *1 Mar* | Bulgaria joins Axis | |
| *3 Mar* | | Capture of German trawler *Krebs* off Norway helps BP break into Naval Enigma |
| *7 Mar* | British forces land in Greece | |
| *17 Mar* | | Hut Three begins sending decrypts to Cairo |
| *24 Mar* | | First Wrens arrive to operate bombes |
| *28 Mar* | Battle of Cape Matapan | |
| *Apr* | Germany invades Yugoslavia and Greece | |
| *3 Apr* | Drawing on Ultra intelligence, Churchill warns Stalin of Hitler's invasion plans | |
| *7 &9 May* | | Capture of weather trawler *München* and of *U-110* helps BP break main naval key, Dolphin |
| *20 May* | German airborne forces invade Crete | |
| *27 May* | Sinking of the *Bismarck* | |
| *22 June* | Barbarossa: Germany invades Soviet Union | |

| | | |
|---|---|---|
| *27 June* | | German Army Russian Front key, Vulture, broken |
| *28 June* | | Cypher materials recovered from German weather ship *Lauenberg* |
| *11 Aug* | Churchill and Roosevelt meet off Newfoundland and proclaim Atlantic Charter | |
| *16–23 Aug* | | Denniston visits USA |
| *27 Aug* | | Capture of *U-570*; with other incidents this leads Dönitz to order examination of Enigma security |
| *30 Aug* | | BP breaks 2 Tunny messages, a vital step in 'solving' the machine |
| *6 Sept* | | Churchill visits BP |
| *15 Sept* | Siege of Leningrad begins | |
| *2 Oct* | Germans launch attack on Moscow | |
| *5 Oct* | | U-boat key Triton, called Shark at BP, separates U-boat keys from German home waters keys |
| *21 Oct* | | Turing, Welchman, Alexander and Milner-Barry appeal for resources to Churchill who replies 'Action This Day' |
| *Dec* | | BP breaks most important Abwehr Enigma cypher machine |
| *Dec 7* | Japan attacks Pearl Harbor | |
| *Dec 12* | Hitler declares war on USA | |
| **1942** | | |
| *Jan* | | New German weather message system ends BP's ability to use weather messages as cribs; Fish machine Tunny broken |

| | | |
|---|---|---|
| *Feb* | | Denniston moves from BP to London; Travis becomes head of BP; 4-rotor Enigma begins service on Shark; black-out on Shark messages follows; first Japanese language course for code-breakers in Bedford |
| *15 Feb* | Singapore surrenders | |
| *Mar* | | Eric Jones joins Hut Three |
| *7 Mar* | Fall of Rangoon | |
| *18 Mar* | | Current reading of JN-25B begins |
| *Apr* | German Baedeker air-raids begin; Rommel begins offensive in North Africa | |
| *May* | First British thousand-bomber raid | |
| *4–6 June* | US Navy wins decisive victory at Midway | |
| *July* | | New Fish section under Tester called the Testery; new Blocks A and B completed at BP |
| *11 July* | | GC&CS permits Enigma decryption in Cairo |
| *Sept/Oct* | | Travis visits Washington; US Navy approves construction of bombes |
| *23 Oct* | Battle of El Alamein begins | |
| *30 Oct* | | Code books captured from U-559 |
| *8 Nov* | Operation Torch: Allied landings in Morocco and Algeria | |
| *Dec* | | Shark broken after 9-month gap; Hollerith tabulating and records section set up in Block C |

**1943**

| | | |
|---|---|---|
| Jan | Churchill and Roosevelt meet at Casablanca; Germans surrender at Stalingrad; Dönitz becomes C-in-C of German Navy | |
| Feb | | Newman forms new Tunny team, Newmanry |
| 1 Mar | | Block E occupied at BP |
| Apr/May | | First machine using valves and relays to deal with Fish, 'Robinson' delivered |
| May | Dönitz orders U-boats to abandon North Atlantic convoy attacks | |
| 17 May | | BRUSA agreement signed |
| 10 July | Allied forces attack Sicily | |
| Oct | Italy declares war on Germany | |
| Nov | Tehran conference begins | |
| Aug | | Block F occupied by Fish teams |
| Sept | | Part of team working on Japanese naval cyphers moves to Hut Eight |
| Nov | | Prototype Colossus machine tried out by Post Office |

**1944**

| | | |
|---|---|---|
| Jan | | Luftwaffe starts to use new rewirable reflector, Umkehrwalze D, with Red and later other cyphers |
| Feb | | Colossus Mk 1 delivered; Canaris dismissed as head of Abwehr |
| 14 Mar | | 4 Colossus computers ordered |
| 1 Apr | | Germans change callsign allocation process and merge Abwehr into SD |

| | | |
|---|---|---|
| *5 May* | | Germans eavesdrop on phone conversation between Churchill and Roosevelt |
| *2 June* | | Colossus II handed over to the Newmanry |
| *6 June* | D-Day landings in France | |
| *13 June* | First V1 hits London | |
| *20 July* | Failed attempt to assassinate Hitler | |
| *Aug* | Allied forces enter Paris; Warsaw rising | |
| *Sept* | | Block H is opened for Newmanry |
| *8 Sept* | First V2 hits London | |
| *Oct* | | Colossus VI installed |
| *Nov* | General Slim begins recapture of Burma | |
| *16 Dec* | Germans launch Ardennes attack | |

**1945**

| | | |
|---|---|---|
| *Jan* | Soviet armies enter Germany in strength | |
| *Feb* | | Germans use complex callsign and frequency changes for Luftwaffe messages |
| *4–11 Feb* | Yalta conference | |
| *Mar* | Allied armies cross Rhine | Luftwaffe messages read again; volume of Fish traffic reaches wartime peak |
| *Apr–Aug* | | TICOM teams from BP seek out cryptographic personnel, records and equipment in Germany |
| *Apr* | San Francisco: drafting of United Nations Charter | |
| *12 Apr* | Death of Roosevelt; Truman President | |
| *16 Apr* | Soviet armies attack Berlin | |

| | | |
|---|---|---|
| *30 Apr* | Hitler commits suicide | |
| *8 May* | VE-Day in the West | |
| *9 May* | VE-Day in the Soviet Union | |
| *May* | | All BP teams required to write accounts of their wartime work; all but 50 bombes are dismantled; only 2 Colossi still in use |
| *21 June* | Okinawa secured by US forces | |
| *26 July* | Labour majority in British election; Attlee prime minister | |
| *6 Aug* | Atom bomb dropped on Hiroshima | |
| *8 Aug* | USSR declares war on Japan and invades Manchuria | |
| *9 Aug* | Atom bombing of Nagasaki | |
| *15 Aug* | VJ-Day | |
| *Sept* | | Travis declares that GC&CS is no longer operational |

# Further Reading

Official histories, to be read critically, are a necessary starting point. See F. H. Hinsley, *British Intelligence in the Second World War: Its Influence on Strategy and Operations*, 3 vols (1979–88) and Hinsley and C. A. G. Simkins, *British Intelligence in the Second World War*, Vol. 4, *Security and Counter-Intelligence* (1990); S. W. Roskill, *The War at Sea*, 3 vols (1954–61); C. Webster and N. Frankland, *The Strategic Air Offensive Against Germany*, 4 vols (1964); J. R. M. Butler, *Grand Strategy*, Vols II, III (1957, 1964); J. M. A. Gwyer, Vol. III, Part 2 (1964); M. Howard, Vol. IV (1964); J. Ehrman, Vols V and VI (1956); and S. W. Kirby, *The War Against Japan*, 4 vols (1957–65); M. Howard, *British Intelligence in the Second World War*, Vol. 5, *Strategic Deception* (1990); J. Jackson and F. Birch (eds), *Official History of British Sigint, 1914–1948* (2010); and Patrick Mahon, *Naval Enigma: The History of Hut 8, 1939–1945*, long secret histories at last published in books.

Compare the official histories of other Allied countries, S. E. Morison, *The History of United States Naval Operations in World War II* (15 vols, 1947–62); W. L. Craven and J. L. Cate (eds), *The Army Air Forces in World War II*, (6 vols, 1948–55); A. M. Leighton and F. W. Cookley, *Global Logistics and Strategy, 1940–1945* (2 vols, 1959, 1968); M. Matloff, *Strategic Planning for Coalition Warfare, 1941–1942* (1959); and D. M. Horner, *High Command: Australian and Allied Strategy, 1939–1945* (1988).

See also M. Howard, *The Mediterranean Strategy in the Second World War* (1964); W. J. R. Gardner, *Decoding History: the Battle of the Atlantic and Ultra* (1999); E. W. Low (ed.), *Changing Interpretations in Naval History* (1950); F. C. Pogue, *The Supreme Command* (1954); G. M. Stoler, *Allies and Adversaries: The Joint Chiefs of Staff, the Grand Alliance and US Strategy in World War II* (2000).

Another two official or authorized histories cover intelligence in detail over longer periods since the Second World War, C. Andrew, *The Defence of the Realm: An Authorized History of MI5* (2009) and K. Jeffery, *MI6:*

*The History of the Secret Intelligence Service 1909–1949* (2010). See also B. Collier, *Hidden Weapons: Allied Secret or Undercover Services in World War II* (1982); R. Absolum, *Die Wehrmacht im Dritten Reich* (3 vols, 1966–71); L. F. Ellis, *Victory in the West* (2 vols, 1962–8); and B. Farrell, *The Basis and Making of British Grand Strategy, 1940–1943: Was There a Plan?* (2 vols, 1998).

For Intelligence see C. Andrew's highly readable *Secret Service: The Making of the British Intelligence Community* (1985); Andrew and D. Dilks (eds), *The Missing Dimension: Governments and Intelligence Communities in the Twentieth Century* (1984); N. West, *GCHQ: The Secret Wireless War, 1900–1986* (1986); R. J. Aldrich, *GCHQ: The Uncensored Story of Britain's Most Secret Intelligence Agency* (2010); A. Clayton, *A History of the Intelligence Corps* (1993); and K. G. Robertson (ed.), *British and American Approaches to Intelligence* (1987).

Books on BP included as essential reading are: F. W. Winterbotham, *The Ultra Secret* (1974) which, despite its mistakes and omissions, was the first book to break taboos; R. V. Jones, *Most Secret War* (1978) which tells with exuberance the story of scientific intelligence between 1939 and 1945; R. Lewin, *Ultra Goes to War* (1978), the first independently researched book on Enigma by an outsider; P. Calvocoressi, *Top Secret Ultra* (1980 and rev. edn 2001), a well-focused insider's account, to be supplemented by his *Threading My Way* (1994); F. H. Hinsley and A. Stripp (eds), *Codebreakers: The Inside Story of Bletchley Park* (1993), another highly readable history of BP which relies on information by people who worked there and pays due attention to other aspects of BP besides the breaking of Enigma; M. Smith, *Station X: The Codebreakers of Bletchley Park* (1998), a book associated with a popular television series; H. Sebag-Montefiore, *Enigma: The Battle for the Code* (2000), a revisionist study which concentrates on naval battles (and captures of codes) and their effects on what happened inside BP; and M. Smith and R. Erskine, *Action This Day* (2001), a series of pieces, admirably chosen, which illuminate all aspects of life and work inside BP. For Colossus see B. J. Copeland and others, *Colossus* (2006).

Sebag-Montefiore, a descendant of the Leon family who owned Bletchley Park in the nineteenth century, notes in his acknowledgements that his book would not have been written had it not been for the publication of Robert Harris's novel *Enigma* (1995) and the West End production of Hugh Whitemore's play *Breaking the Code* (1986). BP by then was becoming identified not with secrets but with drama. For secrecy see J. Vincent, *The Culture of Secrecy: Britain, 1932–1998* (1998); R. Thomas, *Espionage and Secrecy: The Official Secrets Acts of Britain, 1911–1989* (1991); and N. Wilkinson, *Secrecy and the Media: The History of the UK's D-Notice System* (2009). See also D. Kahn, *Hitler's Spies* (1978); H. Skillen, *Spies of the Airwaves* (1989); and R. L. Benson and R. Warner, *Venona: Soviet Espionage and the American Response, 1939–1957* (1997).

There were, of course, writers of books who were to be accused of giving away too many secrets. Gordon Welchman's *The Hut Six Story* (1982) is a piece of non-romantic story-telling which everyone associated with Hut Six would regard as authoritative. In a later edition, however, published in 1997 after his death in 1986 and edited by Stripp, material is added about the Polish contribution to the breaking of Enigma. His old pupil, John Herivel in his *Herivelismus and the German Military Enigma* (2008), gives the fullest account in English of the Polish contribution to our understanding of the Enigma machine and of how it was possible to break it. Among the books that Herivel cites are G. Bertrand, *Enigma ou la plus grande énigme de la guerre, 1939–1945* (1973), which predated Winterbotham but did not create an equal stir in France or outside as Winterbotham did; J. Garlinski, *Intercept: The Enigma War* (1979); and W. Kozaczuk, *Enigma: How the German Machine Cipher was Broken* (1984). See also C. A. Deavours, *Breakthrough 1932: The Polish Solution of the Enigma* (1988).

For BP's code-breaking in historical perspective see the great work to which I owe a considerable debt, D. Kahn, *The Codebreakers: The Story of Secret Writing* (1967, rev. edn. 1996) and his *Seizing the Enigma: The Race to Break the German U-Boat Codes, 1939–43* (1991). I also owe a great debt to Martin Gilbert and his monumental *Winston Churchill*, 8 vols (1966–88) with his accompanying documentary volumes and his general volume *The Second World War* (1989). See also S. Budiansky, *Battle of Wits: The Complete Story of Code-Breaking in World War II* (2000).

For assessments of the value of Enigma in particular places and at different times during the Second World War see J. Rohwer, *The Critical Convoy Battles of March 1943* (1977, English translation from German of 1975); P. Beesly, *Very Special Intelligence: The Story of the Admiralty's Operational Intelligence Centre, 1934–1945* (1977; with new introduction and afterword, 2000); and R. Bennett, *Ultra in the West: The Normandy Campaign 1944–1945* (1979) which he followed up ten years later with

*Ultra and Mediterranean Strategy 1941–1945* (1989) and five years after that with *Behind the Battle: Intelligence in the War with Germany, 1939–1945* (1994). See also G. Pidgeon, *The Secret Wireless War* (2003): and R. A. Ratcliff, *Delusions of Intelligence: Ultra and the End of Secure Ciphers* (2006). See also J. C. Masterman, *The Double Cross System in the War of 1939–1945* (1972).

For the Y Service see A. Clayton, *The Enemy is Listening: The Story of the Y Service* (1980); and K. Macksey, *The Searchers: Radio Intercept in Two World Wars* (2003). There are interesting papers concerning the Y Service and BP matters in H. Skillen, *The Enigma Symposium* (1993) and *The Enigma Symposium* (1994).

For Anglo-American relations see J. Richelson, *The Ties That Bind: Intelligence Cooperation between the UK and USA* (1986); B. F. Smith, *The Ultra–Magic Deals and the Most Secret Special Relationship* (1990); A. H. Bath, *Tracking the Axis Enemy: The Triumph of Anglo-American Naval Intelligence* (1998); and E. J. Drea, *Macarthur's ULTRA: Codebreaking and the War Against Japan, 1942–45* (1992).

For aspects of the war against Japan see A. J. Stripp, *Code-Breaker in the Far East* (1989); C. Boyd, *Hitler's Japanese Confidant: General Oshima Hiroshi and Magic Intelligence, 1939–1945* (1993); S. A. Maneski, *The Quiet Heroes of the South Pacific Theater: An Oral History* (1996); F. B. Rowlett, *The Story of Magic: Memoirs of an American Cryptologic Pioneer* (1998); and M. Smith, *The Emperor's Codes: Bletchley Park and the Breaking of Japan's Secret Ciphers* (2000).

There are now so many articles on wartime BP that there is only space for a few of them to be picked out here. See, however, in book form R. Bennett's collection of his own articles, *Intelligence Investigations: How Ultra Changed History* (1996) and R. Denniston (ed.), *Thirty Secret Years: A. G. Denniston's Work in Secret Intelligence, 1914–1944* (2007). Among individual articles see E. Harrison, 'British Radio Security and Intelligence, 1939–43', *English Historical Review*, 2009; W. K. Wark, 'Cryptographic Innocence: The Origins of Signals Intelligence in Canada in the Second World War', *Journal of Contemporary History*, 1989; C. Andrew, 'The Growth of the Australian Intelligence Community and the Anglo-American Connection', *Intelligence and National Security*, 1989; P. W. Filby, 'Bletchley Park and Berkeley Street', *ibid.*, 1988, D. Reynolds, 'The Ultra Secret and Churchill's War Memoirs', *ibid.*, 2005; G. Jukes, 'The Soviets and Ultra', *ibid.*, 1988; and R. Erskine, 'When a Purple Machine

Went Missing: How Japan Nearly Discovered America's Greatest Secret',
*ibid.*, 1997; and R. Erskine, 'The Holden Agreement on Naval Sigint: The
First BRUSA?', *ibid.*, 1999. Articles in *Cryptologia* include G. Bloch and R.
Erskine, 'The Dropping of Double Encipherment' (1986); W. Bundy,
'Some of My Wartime Experiences' (1987); W. Clarke, 'Bletchley Park,
1941–1945' (1988); G. Bloch, 'Enigma Before Ultra: Polish Work and the
French Connection' (1988, 1989); R. Erskine, 'The First Naval Enigma
Decrypts of World War II' (1997); D. H. Hemar, G. Sullivan and F.
Weierud, 'Enigma Variations: An Extended Family of Machines' (1998);
and D. Davies, 'The Bombe: A Remarkable Logic Machine' (1999).

There are many personal memoirs, sometimes highly selective and not
always accurate accounts, describing how the authors themselves lived and
worked at BP. Several of them, admitting ignorance of exactly what they
and others were doing, nonetheless speculate about the work of the Park
as a whole. By far the best is J. Thirsk, *Bletchley Park: An Inmate's Story*
(2008), which includes seventy-one pages of useful biography of significant
people working at BP, all of them then dead. Among the memoirs are I.
Young, *Enigma Variations: A Memoir of Love and War* (1990, rev. edn,
2000); G. Ballard, *On Ultra Active Service* (1991); I. Roseveare, *Things I
Remember* (2005); G. Watkins, *Cracking the Luftwaffe Codes* (2006); D.
Luke, *My Road to Bletchley Park* (2007); M. Batey, *From Bletchley with
Love* (2008); C. Lamb, *I Only Joined for the Hat* (2008); and P. Shanahan,
*The Real Enigma Heroes* (2008). There are two general books which deal
with the life and leisure of BP inmates – M. Hill, *Bletchley Park People:
Churchill's Geese Who Never Cackled* (2004); and S. M. McKay, *The Secret
Life of Bletchley Park* (2010).

Autobiographies and biographies concerned in part with BP include
K. Philby, *My Silent War* (1968); R. Jenkins, *A Life at the Centre* (1991);
J. Cairncross, *The Enigma Spy: The Story of the Man Who Changed the
Course of World War Two* (1997); M. Drabble, *Angus Wilson: A Biography*
(1995); P. Fitzgerald, *The Knox Brothers* (1977); S. Hampshire, *Innocence
and Experience* (1989); L. Marks, *Between Between Silk and Cyanide: A
Codemaker's War, 1941–1945* (1999); M. Batey, *Dilly: The Man who Broke
Enigma* (2010), the BP life of Dilly Knox; N. Lacey, *A Life of H. L. A. Hart:
The Nightmare and the Dream* (2004); G. Bennett, *Churchill's Man of
Mystery: Desmond Morton and the World of Intelligence* (2007); A. Sisman,
*Hugh Trevor-Roper: The Biography* (2010); M. Mueller, *Canaris: The Life
and Death of Hitler's Spymaster* (English translation, 2007); J. C.

Masterman, *On the Chariot Wheel* (1975); T. Bower, *The Perfect English Spy: Sir Dick White and the Secret War, 1935–90* (1995); and P. Beesly, *Very Special Admiral: The Life of Admiral J. H. Godfrey* (1982).

For SOE see M. R. D. Foot, *SOE in France* (1966); *SOE in the Low Countries* (2001); *Open and Secret War, 1938–1945* (1991); *Foreign Fields: The Story of an SOE Operative* (1997); and (ed.), *Secret Lives: Lifting the Lid on Worlds of Secret Intelligence* (2002). See also W. J. M. Mackenzie, *The Secret History of SOE: The Special Operations Executive, 1940–1945* (2000).

Among narratives of the events of World War II the following are pertinent: Dwight Eisenhower, *Crusade in Europe* (1948); Heinz Guderian, *Panzer Leader* (1950); W. S. Churchill, *The Hinge of Fate* (1951); Chester Wilmot, *The Struggle for Europe* (1952); D. Howe and J. Reeves (eds), *The War of 1939–1945* (1960); J. W. Wheeler-Bennett, *Action This Day* (1968) and *The Nemesis of Power: The German Army in Politics, 1918-1945* (2nd edn, 1967); B. Liddell Hart, *The History of the Second World War* (1970); D. Dilks (ed.), *The Diaries of Sir Alexander Cadogan, 1938–1945* (1971); M. Hastings, *Bomber Command* (1979) and *Overlord: D-Day and the Battle for Normandy* (1984); D. van der Vat, *The Atlantic Campaign: The Great Struggle at Sea 1939–1945* (1990); J. Keegan, *The Second World War* (1990); R. Overy, *Why the Allies Won* (1995); E. Davidson and D. Manning, *Chronology of World War II* (1998); A. Beevor, *Stalingrad* (1994) and *Berlin: The Downfall, 1945* (2002); and A. Daneher and D. Todman (eds), *War Diaries 1939–1945: Field Marshal Lord Alanbrooke* (2001).

For material in the National Archives (which now incorporates the Public Record Office), not updated, see J. D. Cantwell, *The Second World War: A Guide to Documents in the Public Record Office* (1992).

# Index